Thomas G. Norton

South Korea: My Adventures and Sermons

Thomas G. Norton

South Korea: My Adventures and Sermons

Fromm Verlag

Imprint

Cover image: Vom Autor bereitgestellt

Publisher:
Fromm Verlag
is a trademark of
International Book Market Service Ltd., member of OmniScriptum Publishing Group
17 Meldrum Street, Beau Bassin 71504, Mauritius

Printed at: see last page
ISBN: 978-620-2-44060-8

Contents

Preface

How Did My Korean Adventures Began?

They began totally by accident.

I was reading a monthly church magazine and stumbled upon an advertisement. The South East Asia Mission was looking for seven Swiss pastors for an exchange program to go to Japan and Korea in October 1997. This trip would be during the school autumn vacation and I had no confirmation classes or worship services. I was completely free from official church activities. I always wanted to go to Japan so I thought this might be a great opportunity to visit this country. I knew my wife, as president of the Home Help Services in the Canton of Berne, was going to Boston for a two week Conference during that time. My exchange program would be three weeks and our trips would overlap each other. Therefore, I asked her what she thought. She said I should apply for one of the positions. I called the Mission that Friday afternoon and was told if I was interested I should send in my application immediately, since they would be making their selection the following Friday. Then the director added that the Japanese exchange pastor had already been designated. At first I was disappointed, but I thought Korea might also be interesting. I had never been interested in Korea before, even though I had some connection to it.

As a child living in Anchorage, Alaska, I experienced the Korean War from 1950 to 1953 in a small way. During the three war years, my father was part of the Alaska Civil Defense and every Saturday at 6 PM, he went into the basement and used his short wave radio to communicate with other Civil Defense personnel throughout Alaska. They kept in contact with each other in case war broke out or in the event they could help if any emergency occurred. During this time, we often had air raid drills. We were required to turn off all our house lights, close the shutters and pull down our curtains making sure everything was dark so bombers could not see the city. Elmendorf Airforce Base and Fort Richardson Army Base were located in the Anchorage vicinity making Anchorage a vulnerable area for possible attacks.

Anyway, the next Monday I sent in my profile and waited with anticipation for ten days until I received the results. The outcome was positive; I would be one of the six pastors chosen from Switzerland to go to Seoul that fall. Since I was the only one whose mother tongue was English, I was selected as the spokesperson for the group. Now I had to prepare myself with the writing of sermons, getting some knowledge of their language and learning a little about their country.

Soon my adventure began. Here is my story.

My Korean Adventures

Thomas G. Norton, Rev.

토마스지 노튼 목사

안녕하십니까

These lines portray some highlights and experiences while living and working in Korea (한국). (Korea = South Korea) From October 1997 until October 2013, I spent several months almost every year in this land of the "Morning Calm" as it is known. My entire time in Korea was full of unbelievable impressions, encounters and adventures. This outline also describes the Salvation Medical Mission and its ship "Salvation", our daily work and our lives as missionaries on the "Salvation" and on Palgum Island (팔금 도), where our Mission Center was located. During my study leave in the summer of 2000, my main responsibilities were ministering to the islanders and preparing a DVD written in English and German. It describes the country and the South East Asia Mission's endeavors.

The Ship "Salvation" and Its Mission

This Mission operated by the Presbyterian Church of Korea (PCK) was then part of the South East Asia Mission, which no longer exists. Now it is part of Mission 21 and is called the Ocean Medical Mission instead of the Salvation Mission. The Mission Center today is no longer on Palgum Island but instead on the second largest island in Korea, Keoje Island (거제 도). The Mission Center on Palgum now operates an English school for elementary and secondary students.

The ship "Salvation" was our main source of transportation for the volunteer and subsistent paid doctors, Nurses and pastor. Built in 1995 it weighs 40 tons and measures 4.7 meters wide by 25 meters long. It travels every year from March to November through the South Sea (Korean Strait) and the Yellow Sea, visiting more than 100 inhabited islands. Most of the 480 islands are uninhabited. There are roughly 300,000 inhabitants living in approximately 93,550 households. Generally one island is visited daily, but some islands have only a dozen or so residents, therefore two or three islands are visited those days. Bigum (비금 도) Island is the largest and has a population of about 4,000. It is given medical aid for generally three days. Unfortunately not all islands can be visited since they only have a handful of residents. When villagers are unaware of our arrival loud speakers, from the church or community center, are often used to attract attention. During these visits not only medical services are offered but also the Gospel is presented to the islanders.

Christian churches in Korea have worship services every morning, beginning about 4:30 or 5:00 AM. This is also part of our program on the "Salvation" and on Palgum Island, where we permanently resided in the Mission House; however our staff meets for worship services later at 7:30 or 8:00 AM.

Generally, there are about 20 to 50 elderly looking women and few men who are treated. Most of them, especially the women, work daily in the cold seawater and unfriendly weather. They prepare the nets by inlaying them with algae sprouts and setting them in the sea for growing. These patients often suffer from colds, pneumonia and rheumatism or arthritis.

The available medicine has frequently expired or soon will expire since medical institutions often donate it. Sometimes medical equipment might be old or outdated. With financial aid however, updated medicine and new medical utensils are purchased.

It is not only important that these islanders are spiritually and physically healthy but these isolated areas need to be economically healthy. Thus, they need to produce enough goods for personal use and for exporting. Onions, garlic, peppers, seaweed, and some grains are cultivated. In addition, fish, shrimp and other sea animals and plants are found in abundance. Salt as well is produced by extracting it (NaCl) from the seawater. If the islanders are not able bodied they cannot produce. Therefore our job is to keep these folk strong and fit.

Prayer after Medical Treatment

Usually before administering medical treatments, a sermon or meditation is offered. Sometimes a medical lecture on blood pressure, Asian medicine or something similar will also be presented. These talks are determined by the space we are allotted, the amount of time we have and the number of patients we serve. Because we often have only one room, all procedures occur there. This does not seem to bother the patients even though many are only half dressed. One time we put up a curtain for privacy and no one used it. On these small islands, most patients know each other and they are often related.

In these areas, there are almost no medical services, and what is available is often insufficient. Skillful doctors and well-equipped hospitals are on the main land. In large cities such as Seoul, health services in most cases can be compared to the best in the world. However hospital insurance is poor. Only about 50% of the incurred expenses are paid by insurance. Never the less, hospital bills are also considerably smaller. Unfortunately, many people cannot afford doctors and if they can their entire savings are frequently depleted. Retirement benefits are poor or non-existent. Because children are responsible for their aged parents they must also financially support them if necessary, which is most of the time. People in Korea are always surprised that my children do not give me an allowance at my age!

Bloodletting is the surgical removal of a patient's blood useful for therapeutic purposes. Especially the elderly ask for this method even if it is not necessary. On one occasion, a 10-year-old boy was diagnosed as having appendicitis. The doctor used a similar bloodletting procedure by pricking the boy's thumb letting blood squirt five or six feet across the room. This practice had no benefit in this case. The doctor used this procedure because the father was older than he was and if he had not used this technique, the father would not have let the doctor complete the examination. An older person is always respected and he could lose face if his subordinate, in this case the very young doctor, did not accept his suggestion. That afternoon the boy was taken by ferry to a mainland hospital for surgery.

Because money is scarce on the islands, ministers are often paid with farm products and other commodities or services, which we also experience as medical missionaries. After our day's voluntary work we are always offered a nice dinner and during the day lunch and refreshments. On Palgum Island, I often volunteer to read English Bible stories to children. One child's mother is a barber and after the stories, she cuts my hair in her shop.

An island or country pastor earns only $1000/month or less. In a big church in the city, he earns maybe $2000 to $3000, maybe more. Ministers have free housing and many paid expenses. Even more interesting, pastors pay no taxes! Average Korean salaries range from $1000 to $3000/month; this can also fluctuate.

One evening we worked longer than usual and in the darkness could not go from our island back to the "Salvation" with the dingy. It would have been too hazardous maneuvering through the water with the thickly distributed algae lines without destroying this crop. Thus, we stayed on the island and slept on the floor in the room we had used for our clinic. We threw a few blankets on the floor and the six of us laid there all in a neat row. The women slept on the floor in the manse. Anyway, usually people sleep on the floor. Floor heating is normal in Korea, (Koreans invented floor heating long ago, as I was told), but floor heating could cause unexpected problems.

Koreans regularly give gifts to guests no matter what the occasion. Even if someone does not invite an individual, small presents are often made randomly. Therefore, I always have Swiss chocolate in my suitcase to reciprocate. Unfortunately, after leaving my chocolate filled suitcase on the floor I discovered a sweet smelling melted mess throughout my luggage! Sadly, it took one or two more of these episodes before I learned my lesson! Now I wrap chocolate in plastic and if possible do not put it on the floor!

Patients are generally prayed for immediately after their treatments. However one evening after work, we arrived back at the "Salvation" at about 10 PM, and then gathered in a circle on the main deck sitting on the floor. We discussed the patients, each of us receiving two or three personal reports. At this point, we all prayed verbally for our personal patients.

Vocal praying for Koreans is the same as silently praying for westerners. Korean praying distracts me; I cannot focus when listening to vocal prayers! The next morning at my meditation, we prayed silently.

Churches have Wednesday evening services, hence we left our work that afternoon a little early, went back to the ship, ate hurriedly and at 6:20 PM I was informed I had the island sermon at 7:00 PM. It all went painfully fast but this is Korea! Always expect the unexpected! Anyway, I got ready as hastily as possible and was even halfway presentable but with no white shirt and only blue jeans! At 6:59 PM, we finally reached the church after a seven-minute dingy ride and a four-minute walk from the dingy to the church. It was hot that summer evening and I was perspiring but at 7 PM sharp, the church service began. After the service, I passed around unmelted Swiss chocolate! The young people were extremely happy. For many older Koreans, western candy is often too sweet.

In my early days in Korea many young islanders had never seen a westerner, thus after this church service my autograph was requested! This has happened several times since then and I am not even a pop star, but I am white!

On one occasion, after our medical/mission work on one island was finished, we were invited to an afternoon snack. Suddenly I was requested to go into the adjacent room and take a shower/bath. Actually, I did not want to go, but I went: how embarrassing! Anyway, it was a hot day and I was again perspiring, maybe I had an unusual fragrance! Oddly enough, Asians perspire less or differently than Caucasians. They eat more vegetables and grains and less meat. In any case, one should not say "no", so I said "yes" to the bath. The host could lose face if he is refused. Well, after my bath, everyone else went in succession into the adjacent room and bathed. I was relieved; maybe my scent was no different from any of the others' aroma!

One time I tried to buy deodorant and could find none in any store. Mi-jung (미정), one of our nurses, took me to a special boutique pharmacy and we found only one deodorant, Nivea!

By the way, one bathes outside the bathtub! Oh yes, there is always a drain in the floor! After one has showered outside the tub, is clean, has time and wishes, he can get into the tub and relax in the warm water. Then the water is clean and still warm. The same bath water can be used a number of times! As the foreign pastor, I was considered the highest ranked guest of the six of us and therefore was allowed to use the bathroom first. On that occasion, I did not use the tub!

On the "Salvation" ship, one cannot regularly shower, because of water shortage. I remember one instance after three or four days on the "Salvation" we all had the opportunity to shower, in sequence, one after the other. It was a one square meter room with a toilet, sink, closet, mirror and a hose for showering. The two nurses showered first and were so happy to wash their pretty long black hair. After bathing, we all felt clean again. One nurse came to me, running her fingers through her shiny hair and said with a big smile, "Smell my hair"! I responded, "Mmmm, that smells soooo good", and she was delighted!

Korean Christians especially in the mission field drink absolutely no alcohol as I was told before I left Switzerland for the first time. "Don't even think about alcohol." Therefore, I followed their instructions. One afternoon we went to the island general store to buy food for dinner. Two elders from a mainland church visited us that evening and helped us shop. In the store they asked me if I wanted some beer with dinner and of course I said "no". Three times, they confronted me and three times, "no". During and after dinner the conservative doctors as well as the nurses all drank a little beer. Therefore, I decided I could too! The elders wanted me to be their beer excuse! They knew that frequently European Christians drink alcohol. Anyway, we all had an amusingly entertaining evening! Moreover, I was actually glad they bought a 6-pack of beer! It tastes good after hot spicy food especially on a warm summer evening. However, I must say we always had fun together even without beer! We were a big happy family. Some Korean Christians do consume alcohol at times, but usually not in public!

These previous episodes depict some of our encounters with the islanders and many of my adventures while living and working in this medical-mission. The island and "Salvation" ship experiences describe in part a missionary's characteristic daily life in these desolate areas.

Anecdotes About Culture, Customs and My Adventures

These Anecdotes are interesting, informative, maybe offensive for some, but also delightfully pleasant for others and for westerners often comical or unusual. I will categorize them.

Food:

At every meal one finds the national dish, "kimchi" (김치), made of celery, cabbage, turnips, cucumber and similar vegetables, which is sharply spiced and fermented. Sometimes miniature fish, clams, shrimp, garlic and different spices are added, which is called "kimjang" (김장). There are 100 types of "kimchi" or more. Many homemakers and mothers have their own special recipes. Koreans say if they did not eat rice and "kimchi" at every meal, they could not live!

Koreans eat much the same for breakfast, lunch and dinner, including rice, "kimchi" and often fish soup. Fish soup is very special in this country. The whole fish is put into the soup: head, fins, bones and often the intestines along with potatoes and/or "dduk", as well as other vegetables. "dduk" (떡) are small rice balls similar to dumplings. The soup tastes good, but all my Korean friends know I do not really care eat what I call "fish bone soup"!

Consuming “Fish bone soup” elicits the worst table manners I have ever seen: Men spit out fish bones on the table and everything else unchewable or inedible – how repulsive! I do not have to tell you what it looks like! Anyway, women do the same thing and I learned how to do it too, but maybe we do it a little more politely than do Korean men!

In addition, rice is served at every meal. Actually, rice is almost the only unspiced food in Korea except for fruits. Often we eat fish soup, sea snails, algae, and many different sea plants and animals. At the table, there are ten or twelve small dishes with vegetables, fish and a bit of meat among other curious tidbits, of which most are sharply spiced. Sometimes rice cakes topped with raw fish are served, “sushi” (수시). Now and then raw fish, mostly tuna, “sashimi” (사시미), is enjoyed. It is expensive but is one of my favorite dishes. Also very popular, especially for picnics, is “kimbap” (김밥), steamed white rice “bap” (밥) with vegetables and sometimes seafood or maybe meat strips rolled in seaweed “kim”, (김). “Bibimbap” (비빔밥) is also very well liked. It is a hot rice dish with five or six vegetables, a raw egg, dried seaweed strips and maybe raw fish or raw meat or something similar.

There are, of course, some meat dishes. One very popular dish is barbequed pork, chicken or beef called “bullgogi” (불고기), which is prepared similarly to a table grill. Also dog stew “gaegogi” (개고기) or more polite, dog soup „poshintang“(보신탕) is sometimes eaten. Dog stew is considered very healthy according to Koreans. Rarely cat stew is eaten in Korea. It is more often consumed in China. Often dogs but seldom cats are found in the open market. After a purchase has been made, the animal is taken from its cage, electrically shocked and killed. It is unpleasant to hear the squealing dog at this time. After it has been butchered it is given to the customer.

“Samgyetang” (삼계탕) is very fashionable. Everyone receives a young whole chicken in a pot of boiling water stuffed with rice and ginseng “insam”, (인삼) roots. This is also one of my favorite dishes and is eaten especially in the winter when it is cold or one has a cold.

On one instance, I even ate “torafugu”, tiger blowfish (*Takifugu ribripes*), an expensive Japanese delicacy, which is extremely poisonous if not prepared correctly. This fish eaten raw can paralyze and kill a human in a very short time. “Fugu” contains tetrodotoxin and is up to 1200 times more poisonous than cyanide. They prepared it correctly for me; I am still alive!

“Fugu” is tasty and so is raw meat! We went to an open market one evening. Our dinner consisted of five or six kinds of uncooked animal protein! After this tantalizing dinner, back at the host’s house we had some “soju”. Then the hostess Hwah-Suk, (화숙 사모님), gave each of us a big horse pill and said it would kill any worms we had eaten in the raw meat!

Shortly after arriving in Korea for the first time, we walked down a street in a little fishing village about 4:00 PM. I was asked what I wanted to eat. I should pick something out, of what I thought was an aquarium. Observing fish in this large tank was very interesting to me especially because of my Biology studies. Well, I imagined they were kidding, so I chose the largest octopus. Five minutes later, we were sitting at the restaurant table eating this half-living animal! Once inside my mouth it wrapped its tentacles around my tongue and his suction cups grasped me tightly inside my mouth! "My goodness" I thought, "I better chew up this thing fast and swallow it before I choke!" I do like to eat these Octopuses "nakji" (낙지). They are very tasty especially with red sauce. For small children, on the other hand, they are dangerous to eat and toddlers are not allowed to consume them.

Another time we walked through an open market and I saw a pile of light brown curious creatures each about the size of the end of a thumb. Others were being boiled and prepared, and another pile was being purchased. My Korean friends told me I should try them but they smelled bad and tasted the same. They were smacking their lips and gobbling them down like popcorn. It turned out they were edible silkworm cocoons (번데기)! The second time I ate them at Solae Port (소래포구) they were not so bad! They are very healthy, high in protein and lecithin, and they lower bad cholesterol.

Sometimes on the menu is a noodle dish, but eating noodles with metal chopsticks is very slippery! Only Koreans use metal chopsticks.

Once we were invited to the home of one of the many poor island families for an afternoon snack. That afternoon we ate among other curious substances, tree roots! The roots, of course, tasted woody and earthy, for me almost impossible to chew and digest. I do not know how the others could chew it; I could not! When I think of how much poorer North Korea is than South, it is saddening! During the Korean War from 1950 - '53, these people ate just about anything they could find including different kinds of roots and other, for us, inedible stomach fillers.

Western confections are too sweet for most Koreans, but recently pralines, pastry and sandwiches have been introduced. "dduk" (떡), is a solid semisweet rice paste candy and is bland for us, but very popular in Korea! A kind of unsweetened "dduk" is used in soups. Happily for tourists, many western foods can also be purchased in Korea. As well as formal western restaurants, there are fast food restaurants such as McDonald's, pizza restaurants, many western ice cream and pastry parlors and of course Kentucky Fried Chicken restaurants. In Kentucky Fried Chicken cafeterias, their chicken is extremely spicy as are most Korean foods. Western society is slowly entering this country.

For dessert, we regularly eat fruit such as Asian pears, "bae" (배). They are not pears, as we know, but rather grapefruit-sized yellow-white tree grown fruits less sweet than an apple but with a similar texture. There are other foreign fruits such as "chamwae" (참외), a smaller, oblong, yellow-white striped melon. They also have fruits we know: apples, bananas, watermelon, grapes, mandarins, dates, plums, strawberries, persimmons etc.

For Koreans fruit is rather expensive and is considered by many a delicacy. All fruit tastes sweet and is very good after spicy hot food.

On one occasion, about ten of us went to a newly opened very nice western restaurant and had a wonderful hamburger steak dinner with all the trimmings and I ate my fill. After dinner, everybody jumped up and said, "Okay, now let's go have dinner!" I asked the silly question, "Didn't we just eat?!" and they said, "No, we haven't had rice yet!"

Dining Traditions

In the United States of America, "double dipping" is not appreciated. In Korea however, at every meal, everyone eats from many small serving dishes. For some even more disturbing is the fact that most of the time, when soups are served often everyone eats from the same bowl, and friends and relatives frequently consume from each other's plates.

Their tradition says, "Eat and don't speak at the dinner table". Today however, many people are table talkers. When dinner is finished, everyone instantly stands up and is ready to leave. Western culture says, "Relax and enjoy chatting after dining". Nowadays however, western dinner culture is also entering Korean homes.

Since all Korean food is sharply spiced, a person's nose frequently runs while eating. According to Korean values, it is impolite to blow your nose at the table, so one sniffles during dinner! I was taught to blow my nose when it was dripping!

Smacking food at the table and burping after dinner — how uncouth! However, by smacking food the flavor improves according to Koreans. In addition, smacking gum improves the flavor they say. By eating very fast and ingesting air one obviously belches, but fast eating shows the hostess how much you enjoy her meal.

When coming back from Korea I am generally a few pounds heavier. Nevertheless, I have an excuse! I was taught to eat everything on my plate. Their favorite expression is, "Just one more!" which means, "Eat a little extra!" When one eats everything on his plate, he signals he is still hungry and if you do not eat more the host's feelings may be hurt. Thus, do not eat all the food in your dish. This tradition comes from the war era, when food was scarce. It was not good if someone went away from the table hungry.

Toilet paper is used everywhere. Once I took this paper from the dinner table. "Certainly this is a mistake," I thought, and as I did so, I heard several voices say, "No, no we need that". Immediately I put these important papers back on the table! Toilet paper is used for everything, including napkins, Kleenexes, for cleaning up fish bones and inedible table chewing's spit on the tabletop, only to mention a few of its uses! These papers are even used by doctors. Other countries, other customs!

Footwear, Gifts and Culture

Because one eats many spicy foods and much garlic “manul” (마늘), toothbrushes are also given as small gifts. In all hotels, there are always free toothbrushes. Also included is a big tube of toothpaste, which all hotel guests use. I have close to 100 such brushes! Often Koreans carry them in their pockets and satchels.

I could almost open a toothbrush and sock store! Shoes, socks, slippers and sandals are part of Korean culture. Whenever someone enters a home, he always takes off his shoes and either goes sock footed or puts on slippers, which are at the door entrance. It is more polite to wear socks or slippers than go barefooted. Since socks always become worn and holey on the floors they are frequently given as gifts. I have about 50 pairs of new unused socks in my drawers: dress socks, sport socks, hiking socks, wool socks, cotton socks, synthetic socks, left/right socks, slipper socks, ankle socks, and other Korean socks including women’s socks and children’s socks!

Large buildings with many people entering and leaving these structures might have fifty, a hundred or more pairs of shoes at the entryway. It is amazing that not more shoes are lost. The reason for their shoe custom might be that vacuum cleaners are not as common in Korea as in the West. Socks seem to keep their floors spotless!

Since Korean’s wear slippers in their homes when they enter the bathrooms they slide out of their slippers and into rubber slipper-sandals which are at the washroom door entrance. Since the restroom floor is often wet from showering outside the tub and the floor may not be 100% sanitary it is not appreciated when the slipper-sandals are worn outside this room.

Sandals are almost never worn in small churches and seldom in other smaller formal buildings. They are generally not appreciated in any formal buildings. Nevertheless young people often wear sandals more commonly today. Because my feet usually perspired in this warm and hot country, I regularly wore sandals, but it was frequently frowned upon when I visited important people or went into significant buildings.

My good friend, Korean brother and manager (has organized most of my major Korean activities), Jeong In-chul (정인철), asked me why I always carry so much paraphernalia in my big red bellybag. Actually, I am sure he knows what it contains. This bag includes reading material, sermons, an umbrella, a camera, sunglasses, Swiss chocolate and/or other small presents, a dictionary, calculator, a note pad, pencils and pens, and often toilet paper, since many restrooms or outhouses especially on the islands have no such paper. Often I cannot take everything in my bag, so what happens if it is raining or I have no gifts!? Often there are extra umbrellas in the area. In-chul expects me to have Swiss chocolate or other gifts for our next visit! I agree with him.

One young lady, Mi-ran (미란), asked me to do her wedding which I happily did. She refers to me as her pastor and considers me her second father also calling me father. In addition, most of my older adult and good friends are formal with me even though I am familiar with them! Children are formal with their parents, as Mi-ran is with me even though we are very good friends. She buys many things for me such as dinners, clothes etc., lets me use her office and computer, and helps me in many other ways. She even designed and gave me a custom-made traditional “hanbok”. She appreciates what I do for her, but I can never repay her. She has a good job and is able to treat me, in many ways, the same as she does her parents. I consider her as one of my Korean daughters. She gives me no allowance (see p. 7/8), but with her help and presents, it amounts to the same. If I did not accept her gifts, she might be saddened and maybe feel rejected.

One must always be careful when making compliments in this country of cultural differences. On my last Korean visit in 2016, I took my wife with me for the first time. We were invited to a very nice dinner in the "Grand Ambassador Hotel" in Seoul. Mary said to the hostess, Hyang Rae (향래), who sat on the other side of the table, that she was wearing a beautiful brooch. Immediately she took the jewelry off and fastened it to Mary's blouse. Mary tried in vain to give the brooch back, for she did not think Hyang Rae should make her this gift. However, Hyang Rae and all the other Koreans sitting at the table insisted Mary must accept the ornament. After a short debate that Mary lost, she happily accepted the magnificent gem, with a natural pearl, which was surrounded with pink coral. She likes to wear it very much, but now is unsure how she should make a compliment. Koreans are often saddened or maybe even insulted if their gift is not accepted.

Drink

"Soju" (소주), which almost everyone outside the church consumes, is their national drink and is normally about 20% alcohol but can be up to 45% alcohol. It is clear liquor originally made only of rice, nevertheless often today other grains or types of potatoes are added. When I first drank "soju", I thought it was rubbing alcohol, but actually it tastes similar to vodka! I just asked for a sip to taste but the waiter brought a full bottle, which I was supposed to drink! I was told later "soju" only comes in bottles. Someone else at the table drank the rest.

"Maekju" (맥주), beer, was introduced into the Asian countries from Germany. Often one of the major three beers is commonly enjoyed: Cass, Hite and OB. The legal age for consuming alcohol is 19.

"Makoli" (막걸리) is a milky white rice drink (rice wine) about the strength of a mild beer. It has been rediscovered and again introduced into the modern Korean society in recent years and has become fashionable not only in Korea.

"Podoju" (포도주), is their wine made out of rice and fruits, which are often plums (매실주) or black raspberries (복분자). Western wine is becoming more popular.

On one of my trips to S. Korea in the summer of 2002, I spent two weeks in learning some of the basics of acupuncture with Han Jin (한진), Korean Medical Doctor (KMD) equivalent to Oriental Medical Doctor (OMD). He also has a Ph.D. in Herbalogy. Part of his instruction to me was in hand acupuncture, for which Korea is known. The book "Koryo Hand Acupuncture" volume 1 written by Tae-Woo Yoo, O.M.D., Ph.D. was the originator of "Koryo Sooji Chim", "Korean Hand Acupuncture". Yoo studied and taught "Body Acupuncture" at the Korea Silroam Institute of Acupuncture and Moxibustion for five years. Because he realized "Body Acupuncture" sometimes caused side effects, pain or might be dangerous he wanted to develop a new method of acupuncture with none of these properties. "Korean Hand Acupuncture" was the result. Thus, part of my mission work on the medical/mission ship "Salvation" was assisting in hand acupuncture and moxibustion.

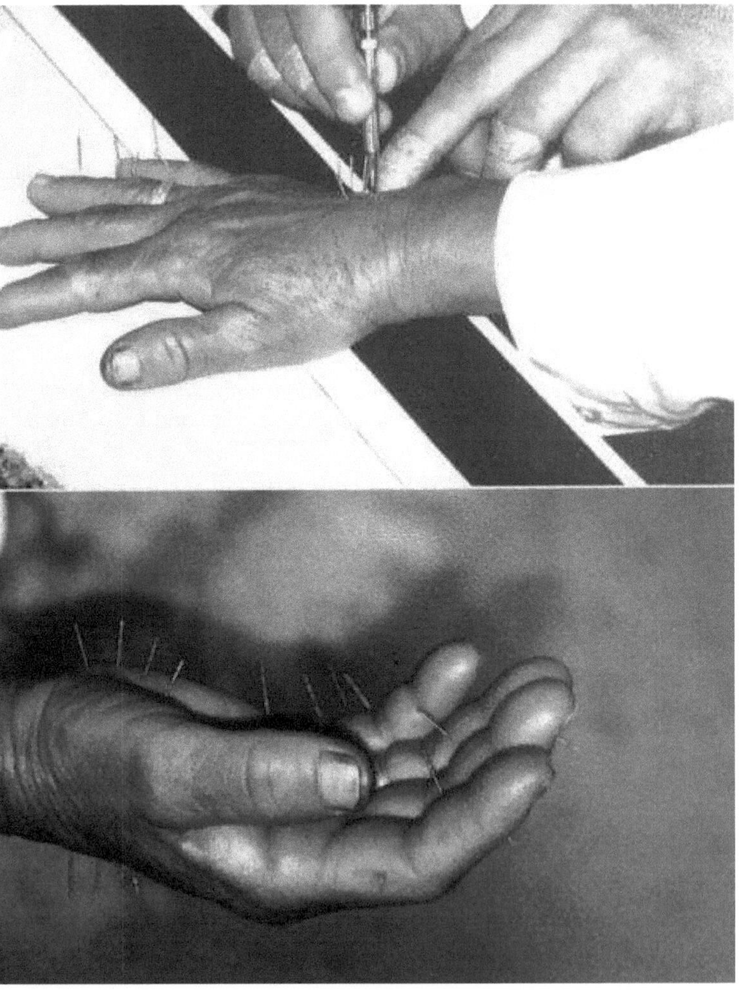

Acupuncture is a procedure in which various-sized needles are positioned in the body for medical treatment. For example acupuncture on the back and shoulders reduces pain in these areas. In the buttocks it relieves leg pain. Sometimes acupuncture is given through the clothes. This has no negative effect as long as several layers of clothes are not worn and the patient does not move. Hand acupuncture eases pain, heals and reinforces the body in many ways as does foot and ear acupuncture. For example smoking can be stopped through ear acupuncture. Hand acupuncture is used in treating arthritis, and other hand and body afflictions. Migraine headaches can be cured through head acupuncture. Forehead and facial acupuncture have positive effects on headaches and facial paralyses. Knee acupuncture helps arthritis and other knee ailments.

"Acupuncture, Moxibustion, Cupping (Bloodletting)"

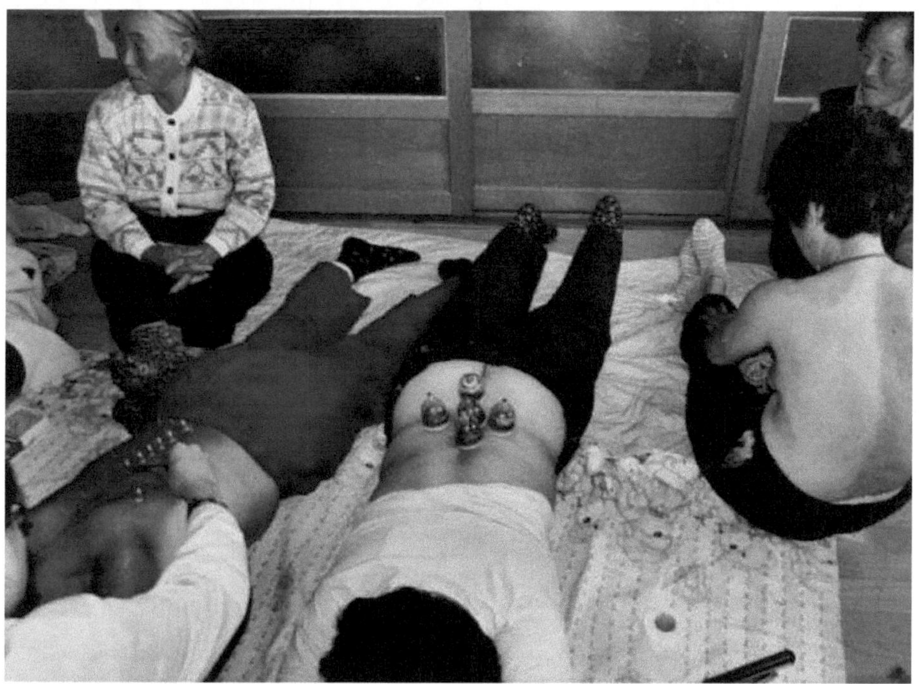

Moxibustion (Moxa) cures many ailments. It also aids in knee acupuncture, in which I often assisted. A "dümm" (뜸) is generally approximately one millimeter long and about as thick as a pencil. A "dümm", composed of a special herbal substance, Mugwort (wormwood), *Artemisia vulgaris*, creates heat when the end is ignited. The Mugwort "dümm" then smolders and releases its substance into the skin.

Moxibustion is used in the patella (kneecap) region, to help heal knee arthritis. An acupuncture needle inserted next to the "dümm" helps the heat penetrate deeper into the knee. Generally two "dümms" are used for one treatment, which extinguish themselves after about ten minutes. The acupuncture needles stay in place ten or twenty minutes longer. The acupuncturist must continually monitor this procedure since the knee area may begin to burn. The "dümm" must then be immediately extracted otherwise scars will result.

Crossing a Street

Driving in Korea can be challenging. Running a red light is common in Korea but the question is, when can one go through red and when not? Evidently, the police do not have a real answer or do not care! Tickets are seldom handed out. Pedestrians have problems at the crosswalks when cars run red lights! A crosswalk without a traffic light can be very hazardous; cars never stop! However, I cross the street in any case! As I begin to cross, my Korean friends say, "no, no, that's unsafe"! I continue, letting the cars know I am crossing by waving my arms. My colleagues continue saying, "Don't walk, stop, stop! It's dangerous!" However, the cars must stop. They do not want to run over a white foreigner, who does not know the unspoken rules! When I am in the middle of the street, I motion for my friends to come across and they do so cautiously!

The church wanted to let me use one or their cars but I said "no". It was too dangerous since I didn't know the unofficial rules!

Waiving down a Taxi

In-Chul and I were almost late for an appointment one afternoon thus we decided to wave down a taxi instead of using the slower buses. Suddenly a taxi drove over to us. I said to my friend, "Isn't it interesting that a taxi came directly to us just as we needed it". In-Chul said he called it over, however I didn't see him hold up his arm and wave to it. He merely, with his arm hanging down naturally, motioned with his hand and fingers for the cab driver to pull up to us. Koreans also motion for someone to come to them in the same way not raising their arms. Many westerners might think you could be calling a pet animal to you. In our world we hold up our arms and wave frantically for a taxi to come!

Karaoke

Music in Korea is very special and important. When living or traveling in this country all Koreans and guests must be able to sing at least one song! Once on an excursion we sang karaoke on the bus. Karaoke is sung often and in many places. Everyone in the bus sang and finally it was my turn. The songs are electronically controlled for judging song quality. The louder the computer clapped, the higher the song quality. I received the quietest claps thus the lowest score. After this failure, I was never again asked to sing!

Unlucky numbers

In the western world, "13" is an unlucky number. I asked a church officer why there was no fourth floor in their building. He said "4", "sa" (사) sounds like the Chinese word "sa mang" (사망) meaning death and is consequently an unlucky number. In a building, often the fourth floor is skipped similar to the neglected 13th floor in the West. In this building, the fourth floor was called "Office"! Of course, most offices are on this floor.

Laundromats

Laundromats are nonexistent in Korea but there are numerous dry cleaners. However many people have washing machines or have access to them. In 2006, I began my work in Shin Kwang Presbyterian Church in Seong Nam. Seong Nam is adjacent to Seoul. In my first apartment, Elder Jeong (정장로님) gave me a brand new washboard to do my laundry! He said I could at least wash my socks with it. However, I said "no". After this "no", The Rev. Kyeong-hee (경희 모사님) donated a washing machine! She and I became good friends.

Suicide

Unfortunately, the suicide rate in Korea is high, especially among young people; it is one of the highest in the world! From elementary schools through universities, every student must be the best according to many Koreans. If a student is not the best, some consider him a failure and he might think he is too. Often only 50% of examinees pass a final exam, sometimes fewer. Often exams are taken two or three times. A Korean expects a lot from himself as well as he does of others. Likewise, a lot was expected from me since at that time I was a permanent resident. Expectations are generally not as high for foreigners.

Often Koreans want to satisfy everyone, thus they compromise themselves. It is impossible to have two positive situations that conflict, for one of these situations may cancel the other. For example having a good quality educational system is positive and so is living a long industrious life. Because of the Korean's high industrial standards, they experience higher success in much of their modern society. However, some students cannot cope with the extraordinarily high educational standards and expectations. Thus, because many fear that they cannot live up to these expectations and because they fear what others might think if they fail, some choose suicide. If one believes he is a failure, committing suicide is easier than losing face! Because of suicide, high educational expectations cancel living a long active life.

Prayer

After a church service one Sunday two or three older adults came up to me along with a college girl. They asked me to pray for her. She was going to take final exams at the university beginning Monday. I generally do not like to accept such requests with so many churchgoers talking and walking past, but it was expected of me. This young lady had studied much and was prepared for her exams but because of society's pressure she was afraid. After my prayer, they thanked me and went on their way. My prayer was not that she could answer all the questions correctly, but rather that she went into the examination relaxed and that she would be able to write the answers she had studied and knew. The next week she came again to church with her parents and one or two others. She had passed her exams and everyone thanked me repeatedly. They said if I had not prayed for her she would have failed. They gave me all the credit and forgot that the Holy Spirit works through many people and in many ways.

Haircuts

An attention grabbing incident arose after a haircut I received in Seoul. I was invited to go into the back room. I am glad I read the book "Culture shock: Korea", a book of Korean customs, given to me by Tina, my daughter. In this back room, a man is offered special services and not manicure or pedicure! This time naturally I said "no" to the offer and lost this unusual service! But did I really lose?!

Another day, I told my Korean brother, Jeong In-chul (정인철) I needed to get a haircut. He told me we could go to a bathhouse. Inside there were two saunas, three big hot tubs as well as both sit down and stand up showers. On one side of the room, there were three or four tables for massages. In addition, there was a section with mirrors for grooming oneself, including towels, toothbrushes and safety razors, combs and brushes, as well as different colognes and lotions, etc. This huge room also included a resting area with TV. At the entrance, there was a dressing area with clothes lockers and on the other side of this gigantic complex, a barbershop. Everyone was walking around naked or with a towel, doing their thing. After my sauna and shower, I walked over to the hairdresser placing my towel on the barber's chair and sat my bare bottom down! I did get a good haircut and I was completely refreshed!

Gayness

When two men walk down the street hand in hand this does not mean they are gay. They are rather good friends and maybe they call themselves brothers. I too have several such Korean brothers. Of course, I feel uncomfortable holding hands and I have told them we cannot do this in the western world. Yet, handholding between heterosexuals and touching among friends is part of Korean culture so when I am in Korea I follow the proverb, "When in Rome do as the Romans". Hugging, on the other hand, is less common although this is also becoming more widespread today.

Sex verification

Confirmation of sex in small children is often difficult, thus adults on rare occasions may touch the private parts of preschoolers for sex clarification. I have observed this touching; it is not considered molestation by them.

Hangul (한글)

During the summer of 2004, I attended a five-week Korean language crash course at the Yonsei National University. (연세대학교) in Seoul. Unfortunately, I was the only grandfather among students between the ages of 18 and 25, who mostly came from American Ivy League universities. My learning ability was disadvantaged since I lived off campus by myself and had no learning connection with the other students. I did not learn as much Hangul for conversation as the other students. I think the school felt sorry for that old grandpa and thus gave him a social promotion!

Ph.D Students and Professorship

Once, I accompanied a professor to a seminar of doctoral students. I was part of the examining committee and was to ask the candidates several questions as well as correct their English. The subject matter was communicated to me a few minutes earlier and consequently I was able to ask the candidates several questions, say a few words and correct some of their English!

In 2008 after I had lived and worked in the Seoul area, teaching adult English, and giving talks and sermons, I was asked to be a professor at the Seoul National University (서울대학교). My courses would be, "English" and "English Bible". Therefore, I filled out the application and everything was fine until they read my age. They hire no one 65 or older, without exceptions!

Tidbits, Zest and Culture

On one occasion during a church senior citizens concert, I was motioned to leave the event. I was then told I had a sermon or speaking engagement somewhere. Soon I discovered it was for university students. As I entered the lecture hall, they were waiting. "Well, that's okay" I thought, since I always had a lecture or sermon in my briefcase. The Boy Scout's motto is "be prepared" and I was always equipped!

If one is not, he cannot respond positively and spontaneously and if he says "no" he is passed by and loses opportunities to participate in diverse events! If you do not risk, you do not win! Yes, you might lose but I have always won in some way and have never really lost. Anyway, by this time I could speak extemporaneously on subjects of interest to all people, if it had to be. I talked about the differences and similarities of Swiss and Korean Churches.

I am glad I have a neck! I bought some dried octopus (오징어) and "makali" on a harbor street in Mokpo (목포) to take back to my apartment for a snack. To make a long story short I lost my wallet! After my snack, I looked for the wallet and it was nowhere to be found. I went back to the harbor street and looked for it on the ground where I had been walking and in the stores where I had purchased the octopus. A man came up to me and asked me if he could help look. Together we searched along the street and he asked the storekeepers but no such luck. He was very friendly and acted as if he knew me. It turned out he was a member of the Yang Dong First Presbyterian Church (영동제일교회) in Mokpo, where I worked for a short time. He called one of the Yang Dong pastors and when he came the two of us went to the police station where we filed a stolen properties report. Rev. Kim gave me 20,000 Won (원), $ 20.00 for dinner. Near midnight, I finally got back to my apartment after about five hours! Then I remembered I took several things out of my pocket before eating my snack. My wallet was among these things, but it had fallen behind the table and was impossible to see. The next day everybody knew I lost my money. I had to tell them I lost it behind a table and I could not find it — how embarrassing! Sometimes I am very forgetful! If I did not have a neck, I would lose my head! Yes, I did give the 20,000 Won back!

My last adventure turned into no adventure! The senior pastor, Rev. Goonyong (군영 목사님) of the First Presbyterian Church, Yang Dong Jee Ill Kyeo Hee (양동재일교회), in Mokpo wanted me to start an extension to his church for English speakers. The position would be for the year 2012, of course any enterprise takes two or three developing and organizing years before it begins to function properly. I only wanted to work a maximum of six months a year but for several years. This was fine with him, but first the Session had to approve this appointment. According to him "they almost always say 'yes'". For me, with the Session now involved, the "yes" would be a "maybe". After that first and only conversation, there was no more response from him or the church! The "yes" or "maybe" turned into a "no". If they had responded to me with "no" after saying "yes", they would lose face. This ethic is unthinkable for Westerners! Even with this "no" answer I had a very good working relationship with Rev. Goonyong and all the staff and especially in the Sunday school department, where I spent most of my time.

Because it is important for Koreans to be the very best, many Korean pastors desire to open their own church. This is very common in Korea, resulting in more than 100 Presbyterian Church philosophies. If a pastor does not agree with a particular church view, he may want to start his own church! It was an honor for me to be offered the opportunity to open an English speaking church. My idea would not have been to split away from the traditional Christian church but to work in this church even if I may have had other ideas. Worshiping together and learning from one another is constructive. Had I been ten years younger I would have said "yes" to the opportunity and accepted the position for a full year, which would then have lasted longer. I do enjoy working in Korea despite the cultural differences. Unfortunately, one gets older and there are other things to do in life before the end comes!

Arirang (아리랑)

There are still many primitive farming methods and poor living situations in Korea particularly in rural areas. However, these industrious people also have many highlights. For example, their standard of living is improving and education is very good. Medicine, electronics, and technical advancements and other scientific developments are some of the highest in the world.

On the other hand, we think of the heartbreaks during the Japanese colonization between 1910 and 1945 and their comfort women. Comfort women were girls and young women, who were forced to prostitute themselves to the Japanese soldiers especially during World War II. One 85-year-old Korean woman told me they had to give themselves to the Japanese soldiers as many as 50 times a day! All Koreans were treated badly during the Japanese occupation, not just women. The Korean unofficial national anthem "Arirang" depicts this and other tragedies: the calamities of war, the few jobs and poor working and living conditions, men leaving home and not returning, as well as other sorrows and misfortunes.

Swimming

When swimming in Korea, women put on their skirt bathing suits that are very pretty and feminine. Over these suits, they put on their street clothes. How refreshing and puzzling for me when now they jump into the water! Korean beaches are becoming more popular but many Koreans still cannot swim. When Koo Kyeong-ok (구경옥) was earning her Hotel Management degree in Switzerland, she was determined to learn to swim. She stayed with me during this time and she did learn to swim.

Men wear T-shirts when swimming. However not I, even though I was offered one and my friends said I should wear it. It was cloudy that day on the East Sea (Sea of Japan) shore and I would not get sunburnt so why wear a T-shirt? After my swim, as I walked out of the water topless, everyone looked at me as if I had sinned, maybe I had for them! The next time I wore a T-shirt!

No Harbor Water

One morning while we were docked and after I had a good night's sleep on the Ship "Salvation", I got up. After looking out the porthole, I saw no water. I could not imagine what had happened. All the other boats and ships were also on dry land, some were tipped sideways. Finally, I realized the tide was exceptionally far out. I had never experienced this and I realized for the first time we had a flat bottom boat!

Hierarchy

Hierarchy in a Korean's life plays a significant role, thus one should always have a business card with him giving all his titles. After exchanging these cards, each person examines them, judges where he stands in this hierarchy and accordingly makes the appropriate number of bows to his counterpart. Today the western custom of shaking hands is becoming more popular. However, only a woman can offer a man her hand if she wishes, which at that time was not common.

Once I offered my hand to a middle-aged woman while her husband was present. Even though we were friends, he became very agitated and told me to take my hand away from her. Later, after he realized this was a western custom, it was okay for me to shake her hand. However, from that time on I was very cautious when meeting especially older women. With young individuals, this is not a big problem. Physical contact in the past has not been the norm. Nevertheless, since western influence, hugging especially among the younger generation is more common.

The elderly, particularly those with white hair, are respected more and have more authority than do others and men have greater influence than women have. Often Korean men wear toupees and many people dye their hair black. I do not wear a wig or bleach my hair but I do tell Koreans I color my hair white so they will have more respect for me! However, I do not know if they believe me! Because I do have white hair and am one of the oldest in our group, tradition says at the dinner table the senior person begins eating first. On my first trip to Korea, I was not aware of this custom for several weeks, thus I always waited for the person at the head of the table to begin eating, and generally, it was a man. Everyone always looked at me to take the first bite. Finally they would said, "Okay you can start eating". Not until I took the first bite did the others begin eating!

Once shortly after arriving in Korea for the first time, I observed a woman open a car door for a man and politely close it after he was comfortably seated! Men can be macho in Korea and this is mostly accepted or tolerated by women. This is part of their hierarchy.

Another time, an elderly woman in the subway train stood up and motioned for me to take her seat. The woman was certainly ten or fifteen years my elder. Finally, I accepted her invitation after other Korean men and women looked at me irritably and insisted I take her seat. Korean woman have a lower position in this man's world, even though western philosophy is slowly entering this country. Some Koreans, especially older men, do not like western ideas. They may have to change their comfortable ways and could lose their power with western influences! However, women control the purse strings! They generally pay for the dinners, buy the food, and do the shopping. Their husbands give them an allowance every month. Interestingly however, often the wife does not know how much her husband earns!

In a bus one time, a woman unexpectedly took the briefcase out of my friend's hand and laid it on her lap without any words. "Hey, that's his", I thought, until I remembered, this is typical when someone is standing with a package and the other is sitting. Words are seldom exchanged and eye contact is improbable. When one of the two leaves the bus or tram the package is given back to the rightful owner. This has nothing to do directly with their hierarchy instead it shows cordiality. Since my coming to Korea, I have witnessed and experienced all these different incidences a number of times.

The Korean dress code is also important to follow. The German proverb "Kleider machen Leute" (Clothes make people.) is especially appropriate for this country. If one is unknown, he should be dressed according to how he wants to be treated. Since I am a Swiss pastor, many church people know me, therefore I am put in a higher category even if I do not always wear a suit and tie. Otherwise, if I dress sloppily and am unknown I will not be recognized and treated as a responsible and respected person, as I have experienced.

Sunday School

"Adult Bibel Study"

In 2006 I began my new job in Shin Kwang Church. One of my main responsibilities was to lead part of the Sunday school. I worked with all ages, from the preschool to the university level. It was quite interesting but very challenging since in Switzerland I had never taught such a wide variety of young people. I never taught children younger than the fifth grade nor did I ever teach university students. Some classes were more than 100 children. In such large classes, often the youngsters became restless. A number of teachers were always present to keep the children disciplined. On the other hand, it was my job to keep the young people interested. Sunny (이대선), one of my translators and a very good friend, helped much with the upper level young people. Kelly (왕경선) helped with the youngest children. She and I also taught together in a public nursery school, which I enjoyed very much. We complemented each other nicely.

Later I was to reorganize the Sunday school department. Therefore, it would be necessary to discuss new options with the teachers and possibly talk to some of the youth. This proved difficult since only I, as the foreign pastor with authority, was expected to make all decisions not considering anyone else. I was now part of their hierarchy.

Military officers rank especially high in the Korean hierarchy. In-chul is a retired Marine Corps Colonel and a church elder, thus he is one of the unofficial highest officers in the church. As an elder (장로님) he can give orders and they are often followed even outside the military.

In any case, now I was to give orders. Elder Jeong told me to reorganize the Sunday school any way I wished: method, time schedule, everything. The department would comply with me, because of my position and in addition, since he would support me. The teachers of course would probably not like this, since they would not be involved in the decision-making. Finally however, I was able to talk with some teachers to a degree. Maybe some did not especially appreciate this, for I was the expert and supposedly knew everything that had to be done. It was essentially my responsibility and accordingly, I had the say. I should do what was right, without consulting the teachers or listening to the children. I was the professional and they would be obligated to oblige me! Such authoritarianism is slowly changing in today's Korean society.

Of course, involving the teachers in the decisions tends to diminish the power of the unofficial authoritarians! Rulers must then share their power with others. Actually, I was put on a high pedestal to be able to be part of this style leadership. Obviously, this is not the western system and was certainly not agreeable with me. I did not accept this position and as a result probably lost some power, but because of my decision, the teachers appreciated me more! Consequently, the teachers developed more courage to say what they wanted. In conclusion, I was able to help reorganize the Sunday school to a subtly small degree with the help of the teachers. We must not forget hierarchy is part of Korean culture and has its own rules that are hard for westerners to understand. Those at the high-end have more say.

Time

Koreans have a different concept of time than Westerners. Once I was supposed to wait 15 minutes in a room. The 15 minutes lasted 75 minutes. Yes, of course I had reading material! In Korea, one must always be prepared and ready to act spontaneously.

On one occasion, a friend was to pick me up at 8:30 AM. Therefore, I knew I had to be ready at 8:00 AM. Well, he knocked on the door at 7:15. Now he had to wait; I was just getting into the shower! On two or three occasions, I have waited and no one has even come. At these times, a communication problem has partly been to blame. In several situations, people have canceled in the last minute. This of course agitates me when my (western) schedule is tight! My Bible classes always start 10 minutes late and then the participants want me to teach longer! The last members come sometimes 20 minutes late. Should I begin my class again every time a participant enters?! It has been difficult to get used to these delays. However, time is different in Korea and one must adjust. Being tardy is not only accepted, but also is probably expected. One pastor friend said I should be lenient. If I started the class 15 minutes later the class members would still be late!

Also Koreans often jump in to help immediately, even if they have little or no time, thus they are late for their next appointment. It is very difficult for them to say "no". They would rather say "yes" and be late at their next meeting. In this case, helping others cancels their punctuality to their next rendezvous. I have learned not to criticize their tardiness since they are often obliging others.

One Christmas Eve I was waiting for the bus near my apartment in Kwang-ju several miles from Seong Nam and my church. The bus was very late that evening, which often happens particularly on holidays. Even with schedules, they are frequently either early or late! At any rate, a car drove by, then stopped and backed up a little. The driver rolled down his window and shouted to me, "Are you Norton "Moksanim" (노튼 목사님) and are you going to the Shin-kwang Church (신광교회) Christmas service". I was late and was happy to accept this ride. I did not know the driver and maybe took a risk. However, if you do not risk you do not win! He drove me 20 minutes to the church, dropped me off and went on his way. Certainly, he was late for his appointment, but he was helpful and I appreciated it!

Another time In-chul, my buddy, and I almost missed our bus stop. We hurriedly exited the bus, but I left the pair of dress pants I had just purchased at the open market under the seat in the bus. With hundreds of busses and thousands of people in the city of Seoul I thought I had certainly lost those unworn slacks. In-chul and another friend called several locations and found a bus "lost and found" bureau. The next day the three of us went by bus three or four hours to this office. At the office under one of the desks my pants were retrieved. There must be dozens of bureaus and offices where lost articles are delivered. If it had not been for my two friends calling many places my slacks would never been found. They spent hours and hours calling around and then finally we went to the right "lost and found" bus station. I thought our time and energy was being wasted since it would certainly be less expensive to buy new trousers. They insisted we would find them. Surely they could have spent their time and energy better. They helped me and probably neglected something more important.

As I experienced on Christmas Eve, busses can be early or late. Everyone accepts this. Their time schedule depends on several things. When someone flags a bus down, often busses stop for people even if it is not their bus stop. One time I got on a poorly marked bus, which was not scheduled to stop at my bus stop. When the driver passed where I wanted him to turn, I told him I should have gotten out several hundred meters earlier. He immediately pulled over, stopped on the highway, and let me out. Usually I could exit the bus only a few hundred feet from my apartment, but this time I had to walk about two miles!

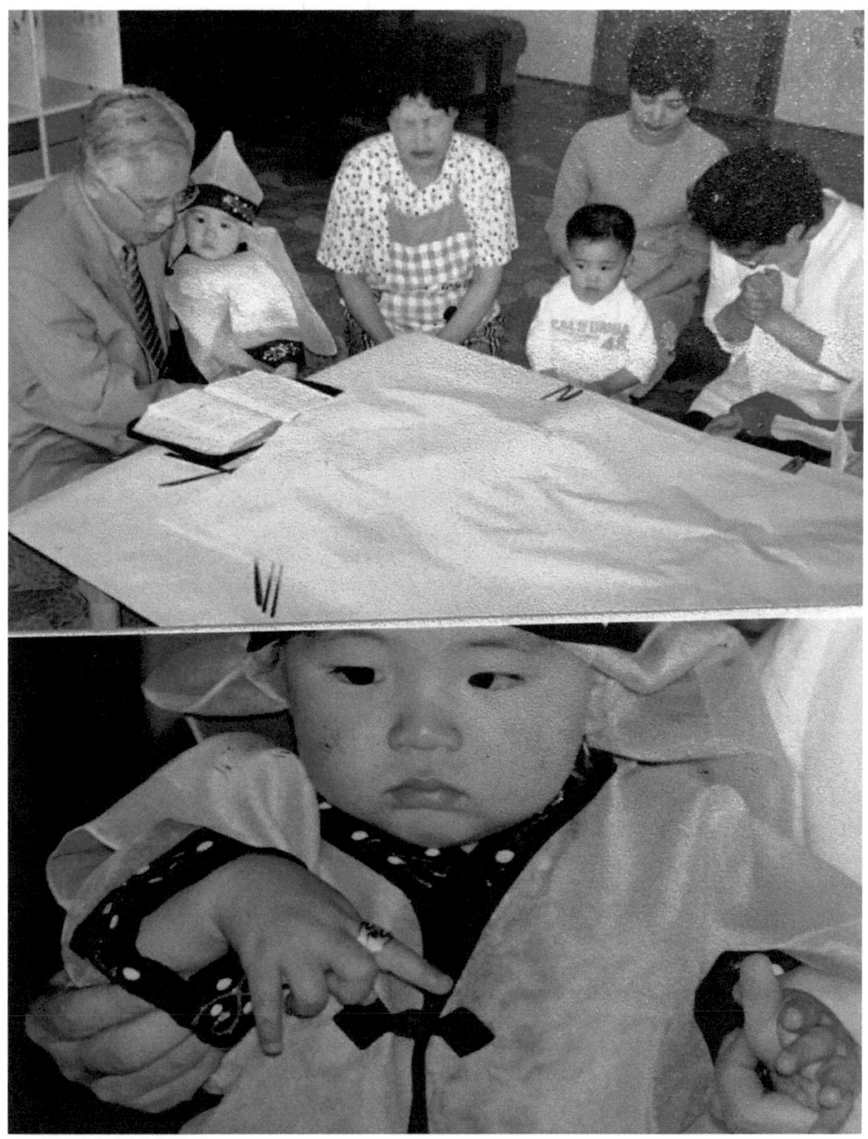

"'baegil' Ceremony"

A baby celebrates his first birthday the day he is born. On New Year's Day, he will be two years old! Thus, if he is born on Dec. 31 he is one year old and the next day, Jan. 1 this one day old baby will now be two years old! If he is born on Jan.1, he is one year old and must wait a year until the next Jan. 1, when he will be two. So, a Korean is between one and two years older than he is by western calculations.

In Korea birthdays change every year because Koreans use the lunar calendar most of the time, which also varies every year. This custom is also slowly changing probably because today one must frequently give his date of birth on applications and other documents.

After a baby is 100 days old "baegil" (백일) is celebrated. The minister blesses and dedicates the infant to God and the church. One could say a "pre-baptism". Life begins with conception and three months after leaving the womb, the baby is one year old. Now the baby is blessed. The determination of the baby's age is somewhat confusing to me.

One Sunday after my Bible class Mi-ran announced we would now have the 100-day blessing for Sunny's (아대선s) baby girl. She was dressed in a beautiful blue "hanbok" (Korean traditional dress; Boys dress in pink.). She gave instructions to us: some were to arrange the room, some to organize drinks and refreshments, and I was to deliver the sermon and bless the baby. I had never done this, but I had observed this celebration once. I was the only pastor there at that time so again I say "Yes". There was no time to think and prepare, so while walking to the meditation room I opened my Bible randomly and there it was, my text without turning another page! The Holy Spirit was present and everyone appreciated the blessing. The Holy Spirit's help always amazes me!

Ethics and Culture of Trip Planning

Experiencing Korean's culture and character are both refreshing and challenging. Sometimes it is difficult for westerners to value their customs and qualities. Because of many variables, it is not possible for Koreans to think, act and be like westerners. It would be rather dull and uninteresting if all cultures were the same.

Also in some instances, Koreans speak English more accurately than English speakers do! When I say to a Korean, "You don't want to go to the store do you"? They answer "yes", because they do not want to go to the store. We speak incorrectly when we answer "yes" and mean we do want to go to the store. A double negative means "yes". This has often caused communication problems between them and me. Also the understanding the meaning of "yes" and "no" resulted in some confusion in our trip planning.

Korean and western business ethics differ. It is often difficult to know what Koreans mean when they say "yes". "Yes" often means "maybe". When they say "maybe", they frequently mean "no". If they answer "no", it is probably an emphatic "no". You probably should not have asked the question. Sometimes their answers can mislead foreigners. They do not realize what they are saying and do not understand that westerners depend on "yes" as being a "yes" and "no" as being "no". This is their culture and we must learn it.

But sometimes a "yes" can turn directly into a "no"! In 2007, I was to organize a 5-day trip in Switzerland for about 30 Korean pastors. The organization began and abruptly ended; they canceled the trip. "Okay that can happen", I thought. Then in Aug. 2008 the program became definite. The trip was organized perfectly on my side, exactly as they wished. Six weeks before the trip was to begin, I called Korea to make sure everything was in order. I was shocked, but on the other hand, for some reason I had an uncomfortable feeling. Their response was, as in 2007, "we don't have enough participants!" Obviously, they had not learned from their first withdrawal. This second cancellation would cost them fees since many Swiss reservations had been made. If I had not called, hotel reservations would have been exorbitant, since the rooms were already earmarked. They probably did not learn from their second annulment either. This was again a shocking experience, but somehow I expected probably another cancelation. I have learned to recognize Korean mentality! Again, "you must expect the unexpected", but also, as in this case, you must expect the expected! These particular Koreans never again tried to organize a Swiss trip with me or with anyone else.

One of my big adventures was in October 2010, a three week Swiss/Korean trip, which brought 15 Swiss to Korea. The biggest adventure was trying to complete this trip efficiently. However we did successfully venture over the heavily guarded Demilitarized Military Zone (DMZ) and went through part of one of the tunnels the North built during the Korean War leading into the South. We were allowed to walk through one of the highly guarded rooms used for eventual meetings between the North and South. It was not permitted to touch anything in the room or shake the hands of North Korean guards and it was not tolerated to smile at or make any eye contact with them.

In addition, we visited Korea's largest and extremely beautiful Jeju Island (제주도). The first time I visited Jeju in October 1997 it was a wedding and honeymoon island. Thousands of Koreans were married there. Today few wedding couples marry in Jeju. With lower costs and better transportation, wedding paradises are available in many other parts of the world.

Anyway, it was impossible to organize and execute our church trip with our chosen travel agency. We were not able to find common working grounds to do business. Business ethics in Korea differ from those in the western world. Cultural and language barriers also presented complications. The Swiss wanted detailed information to print a program and the Koreans could not deliver this information, even though I provided much material and gave them several time extensions. They said "yes" they would deliver the data but were unable to do so. I think the agency from the beginning did not intend to provide us the needed program information. Their "yes" was actually "no". Unfortunately, as a result, I had to cancel our working relationship with them. We even tried to use a Korean travel agency in Switzerland; that also failed.

Fortunately, our Swiss-Korean translator Eun-Suk (연숙) Schroeter from Ostermundigen helped us tremendously with the language and cultural differences while in Korea. Considering these complications the trip went extremely well and it was remarkably interesting and educational for both Swiss and Korean participants. We all learned much about Swiss and Korean personalities and cultures. At our last dinner together at the "Outback Steak House" in Seong Nam, several of us gave short uplifting talks about the trip and the Korean organizers Jeong In-chul (정 인철), Choi Kyu-seong (최 규성 목사님) and Uhm Hwah-sook (엄 화숙 사모님), gave to each of us a bottle of personalized ginseng liquor. We all had a nice time that evening and thanked each other for a successful trip. After three weeks, we all had a hard time leaving our newly made friends.

Weddings

Korean Weddings have beautiful performances and awe-inspiring musical interpretations with many brilliant soloists. Often performers and musicians wear their traditional costumes, the "Hanbok". The bride often must save money many years for her wedding. Standard weddings seem to be very commercial costing between $20,000 and $30,000 and generally more than half is spent on bridal dresses and costumes. The bride often has at least two or three beautiful wedding gowns and the groom has sometimes two, seldom more. Their wedding outfits frequently include the traditional "Hanbok" (한복).

After the wedding celebration hundreds of guests are invited to a sit-down dinner in a big dining hall where dinner tickets are sold. Wedding presents are generally substantial cash gifts. The wedding normally occurs not in a church but in a wedding parlor and a pastor often has only a small part in the service. Laypeople also speak. During the wedding ceremony there seems to be much commotion and less religious concern than in most western churches. People walk in and out of the wedding hall during the ceremony since the door is frequently open. Officials and congregation members often talk or whisper with each other in the back of the chamber. Though I have attended many Korean weddings and participated in two, it is difficult for me to accustom myself to the disturbances and the seeming indifference in a Christian wedding.

Cemeteries

Cemeteries are often scattered throughout the countryside. One can see mounds of dirt one to three meters high or even small hills. Sometimes there are knolls several hundred feet high. Similar to the pyramids in Egypt the height and size of the grave is determined by the importance of the deceased person.

"Ordination of Elders"

Church and Sermons

The first day I arrived in Korea, October 8, 1997, after a long tiring flight, I was asked to deliver a sermon on Sunday in English – no problem; I had one ready. I would preach English from my German manuscript. However, an English text for the translator was required and I was to put the English version on the minister's desk at 8:00 AM the next morning. In order to complete this task I asked for a computer. After dinner as I sat down, I realized all the keys and script on the key board were in "Hangul" (한글), the Korean language. The Reverend ("Moksamin") Choi (최 목사님) changed everything to English and disappeared. Now I could begin but I evidently pushed a wrong key and it was again in "Hangul". Pressing more keys was of no avail. What do I do now – nobody was in the office – I was alone – all the pastors and my Swiss colleagues were having a night on the town and I had to translate a sermon which I now could not accomplish?! After a few more minutes pushing keys, suddenly all was again in English – thank God! Unfortunately I had more Korean computer concerns that evening, but after midnight four hours later I was finished and my body was also completely finished and exhausted, but not from the jet lag – well, maybe a little!

One Sunday, I had two sermons to deliver. After preaching the sermons several church officials and I evaluated them and the conclusion was that the older worshippers appreciated the first, conservative, witnessing type sermon. Generally, those under 40 years of age valued the second type of sermon. It was a more progressive sermon, the central theme being "women and men are equal". Women in Korea are often considered second-class citizens, thus this topic. Such attitudes are changing very slowly.

For one Wednesday evening church service in May 2003 I was fortunate to have the opportunity to deliver a sermon in the Myungsung Presbyterian Church (명성교회) where The Reverend Kim Sam Hwan (김삼환 목사님) was the head pastor. On several occasions I was honored to be his guest. Except for the Full Gospel Church, also in Seoul, this is the largest reformed church in the world with about 1,000,000 members and holding seven Sunday worship services! Myungsung also has seven church choirs each with 600 members! At this evening service, there were 2000 parishioners on the main floor and 1500 in the balcony. It was televised to another church of about the same physical size. This was an amazing experience speaking to such a large congregation and being able to watch myself on television while preaching! In most of the rooms and lecture halls at Myungsung all happenings can be televised.

Once after an evening mediation at 11 PM, I was told my responsibility the next morning at 7 AM was the 30-minute meditation. This was the third day on our exchange trip in 1997 and I had no choice except to respond with "yes", since only I spoke fluent English and was selected as spokesperson for our exchange group. I had no idea what to say, but between my dreams, all preparations were made! The next morning all went well.

Another time while driving from Seoul (서울) to Kwang-ju (광주) about a four hour drive south of Seoul I was suddenly informed I had a welcoming introductory speech to make at the inauguration of a new organic farm. By the time we arrived in Kwang-ju, my speech was ready in my head. The car ride was too bumpy for good note taking. Several agriculture and other officials spoke as did I. At the end of the speeches, we cut the ceremonial ribbon.

The seven of us were handed white gloves to wear for the ribbon cutting. White gloves are almost always worn for Korean traditional events, for official happenings and for special church ceremonies. They are also worn for passing out the bread and wine at all communion services.

One such church ceremony was the ordination of new elders. I was included in this ceremony with about seventy-five other church officials. On other religious and often for secular events I also participated. At this ordination, we were all given white gloves to use for the laying on of hands and for blessing the more than 100 new elders as well as for that day's communion service. These ordinations take place every two or three years involving a number of churches.

While working in the Shin Kwang Church (신광교회) in Seongnam (성남) my sermons were of course delivered from the pulpit. Unexpectedly one Sunday I was asked to preach from the baptismal fount beneath the pulpit. This was confusing to me, since I was not informed of the change. During the announcements, I told the congregation ironically this new situation surprised me, but it was better, because I was closer to them and now could see the choir much easier! After the service, a session member told me they voted that only the senior pastor and guest preachers would be allowed to preach from the pulpit. I was no longer a guest pastor, but a church employee. The reason for this change was because unauthorized lay people were speaking from the pulpit. My sarcasm caused much parishioner and session discussion, also resulting in my conversing with several church session members. Consequently, this new decision was revised and my next sermon was again from the pulpit!

Once I suggested I wear my robe but quickly someone said, "A robe is only reserved for the senior pastor". This did not bother me since I did not have my robe in Korea.

I have enjoyed my work in Korea very much, though often it has been very challenging. Because of my independent employment in Korea, I was able to say what I thought and most of the time my proposals were accepted or at least seriously considered. Again, an older person with white hair has more authority in this land of hierarchy!

On most church occasions after the choir sings a song, or the minister delivers a sermon or says a prayer, the congregation almost always claps. I always thought the congregation was to meditate after a prayer or sermon! However, there are other ways to praise God. Being joyous and clapping is also praising God and thanking him.

Important people and people who think they are important always use loudspeakers! Once, a lay pastor was sitting at a small table with two parishioners sitting across from him. I was situated at a distant table listening to his wedding counseling. The minister used a microphone with large church amplifiers while talking to the couple! His voice could be heard throughout the big church. He could have whispered without loudspeakers and still have been equally heard by the couple!

On one Sunday in an island church service with about fifteen worshippers, the singer sang with a microphone and loudspeakers so piercing that my ears ached! Her voice could be heard several blocks away! With fingers in my ears it was still too loud in this small church! Everyone looked at me a little funny but I had no other choice or I would have harmed my hearing! By the way, this attractive lady used to be a nightclub singer!

Conclusion

The Presbyterian Church is the largest protestant church in Korea; in philosophy it ranges from conservative to fundamental. My views are rather liberal compared to Korea's protestant church and I see myself as a modern missionary, a missionary who points to new possibilities and suggests some liberal biblical understandings. I believe I have been able to widen the Korean church's perspectives in a very small way. We have learned from each other and have stimulated each other's thinking through our different customs, philosophies and interests. Also because of their distinctive Christianity, my faith has grown. Many Koreans have shown their concern for me, with their coordinating abilities, their translating skills, and readiness to help. Consequently, with this support I have been able to speak, teach and preach in numerous churches and participate frequently at events in many parts of Korea. I have learned to value this folk, their culture, and special Christianity and have made many lifelong friends. My Korean translators have always helped me in many ways.

As Soren Kierkegaard said you must "take the leap of faith" and this I have certainly learned and done. If I had been afraid and said "no" on many occasions, I would never have had the opportunity to go to so many places and participate in many significant events. I would not have really enjoyed my Korean life. Be positive and with few exceptions say "yes" even if fear arises in you. One can accomplish much more if he really desires to achieve a goal, if he trusts in the Holy Spirit or if he has no other choice.

Koreans are industrious, generous and welcoming. Sometimes they can be arrogant and physically pushy especially if you are unknown to them or if you are in a waiting line. One should not take this personally. This is their culture. Some Koreans consider this arrogance and pushiness as impolite.

Korea is a beautiful country with many opposites. It has a rich antiquity of which the Koreans can be proud; sadly, some of its history is tragic. Today unfortunately, the disadvantaged and handicapped often still live in very poor circumstances and must surmount many difficulties. Many do not know anything else; this is just their way of life!

After all the time I have spent in Korea and in my many encounters with culture and society I do believe Korea is not a country for every person if the individual cannot adhere to the following suggestions. Be continually open for changes and be able to adapt suddenly. Be able to eat many unusual foods most of them being very spicy. Like adventure and the unexpected. Trust and try to understand this folk. Flow with the current and do not think you know more than they. This is their country. They can help you more than you can help them. Be able to adapt and live according to Korean customs, then you will also have an interesting and adventuresome experience in this land of the "Morning Calm" as did I.

감사합니다

I Pulled My Arm Away

Mokpo, Yang Dong Jee III First Presbyterian Church, 25.10.2009

Mission Sunday

Text: Luke 13: 10 - 17
Scripture readings: Exodus 20: 8 - 10; John 15: 12 - 17

I am happy to be here in Yang Dong Jee III Presbyterian Church. I bring you greetings from the Evangelical Reformed Church of Switzerland.

Seven months ago, I was in South Africa and saw the poverty there, especially in the Township slums. I observed many types of diseases, including AIDS, as well as mentally and physically handicapped people. Many of these problems could be solved with better, housing, nutrition and medicine. However, these people are poor, and cannot afford such luxuries, as can most of us. Today, on this World Mission Sunday, I will talk about our Christian ministry in the world, including an experience I had in the Old City of Jerusalem.

In October 1971, I visited the Middle East, one of the most interesting places being Israel. The Old City of Jerusalem was in some ways depressing with its primitive living conditions and many health problems. These health difficulties were similar to those in the Townships of South Africa. I saw blind men standing in the extremely narrow roads of Old Jerusalem, attempting to attract attention. I saw beggars sitting with crossed legs on cobblestone streets. I saw a crippled man squatting against the Wall of Jerusalem at the Gate of Damascus asking for alms as Arabs, Jews, and Christian tourists entered the Old City.

As I walked down one street, which was teeming with Arabs, in their ancient flowing gowns, I began to imagine myself in the same streets as Jesus some 2000 years earlier, and seeing the same sights. There were donkeys piled high with cardboard boxes or loaves of bread and little Israeli children playing half-naked in the streets. One of the most amazing sights was that the entire city was made of stone. Covering many of the walkways were stone arches. Crowded together on both sides of these walkways were tiny stone stores and shops selling everything imaginable.

The newest parts of the city were about 400 years old and the oldest parts more than 2000. Not only was the city aged, but also the mentality of the people was archaic in many ways. Therefore, technology and medicine still lacked many modern techniques. However, since Israel's independence in 1948 and especially since the 6 days war in 1967, Israel has made great strides forward even though Jerusalem's citizens are continuing to die of curable diseases.

As I continued my walk in the crowded streets, I was shoved into an old, homely, crippled woman dressed in a long black cape. Luke's account of Jesus healing the withered woman reminded me exactly of this woman.

Before continuing the story however, our guides told us to stay away from beggars and not to buy from peddlers because they might pick our pockets or cheat us with their merchandise. We were also told to be careful of what we ate and drank, and to stay away from the sick.

As the crowd pushed me into the old woman, she desperately grabbed my arm with her bony fingers and held tightly. She looked like a witch with her pointed nose and angular face. I can see this woman today.

I was stunned, since I saw precisely this woman in a picture, as a child. It was in a Bible, from which my great-aunt Ora read. I looked for this woman's picture several times after my Old City experience, but to no avail. Maybe I looked in the wrong Bible. Not finding her picture greatly troubled me. It was shocking to me, since exactly this pictured woman I saw!

My reaction was to pull away from her, as fast as I could and I did, though her grip was strong. However, I did not need to pull away; she was not going to make me sick. Instead, she wanted to be healed from her crippled condition and she wanted spiritual health. All she wanted from me was my love and compassion. After the fact, I was extremely distressed that I did not comfort her.

When Jesus healed that withered woman in the village, she did not have to go to him; instead, he went to her. He held out his arms giving her the desperately needed love and compassion. The woman had faith in Jesus and because of her faith, and his concern, she was straightened and made well.

Jesus reached his arms out to the woman, giving her what she needed. I pulled my arm away removing any hope she may have had.

Our responsibility is to go to the poor and needy, not wait for them to come to us. We want to help where and while we can.

It is easy to see why throngs of people came to Jesus. He not only stretched out his arms but he let his followers literally cling to his body sometimes tearing his clothes. The crowds pursued him throughout his entire ministry at times making it nearly impossible for him to be alone in meditation but he never once refused anyone. His love and forgiveness was unconditional and was meant for everyone including the most evildoers. He had no limitations for those he served.

How can we show our love to the poor and needy even if we do not always agree with the way they act or live?

If Jesus had done what some might have expected he would have cast out wrongdoers as being worthless and unable to be forgiven. Instead, Jesus accepted all these people as they were and forgave their many wrongs. Because he forgave individuals like the prostitute and the corrupt tax collector Zacchaeus and because he even forgave those who were about to crucify him, many learned to love and have faith in him. It is our Christian duty to forgive the poor and needy even if they may be guilty. They might not be aware of their guilt and we probably do not know why they did what they did. The Bible says, "Don't judge others". Only through forgiveness can we really help!

Jesus healed the woman on the Sabbath ignoring the ancient Hebraic Law of Moses. He did not neglect the Sabbath or make it unholy with his healing. Yes, the Sabbath was a holy day set aside for rest and meditation. However, as was every day it was a day for doing the Lord's work, for giving oneself to others in love. God's love has no limits. Jesus spread his love in all directions, at all times, to all people. The commandment he gave in those days is also meant for us today, to love and forgive. How can we fulfill this commandment in providing for the sick and homeless?

Since Jesus healed on the Sabbath, the Jews became violently angry and for that reason, and other so-called unholy deeds, he was crucified. He only wanted to spread God's good news of love. He did not fear the murder warnings given him. Others did not influence Jesus. He did what he knew was right even though he made many enemies. He did what he believed and did not let anyone interfere with him. He was not afraid to give himself and help those around him.

As I look back on my experience in the Old City, of what was I afraid? Did I fear the pickpockets, the diseases, or was I frightened I would get lost in the maze of crowded streets? I think it was a little of all this, but I also know I was afraid to express my love to that old woman. I would have felt self-conscious if I had put my arm around her and helped her. She might have taken advantage of me if I had expressed my feelings to her. I could have been made vulnerable emotionally. Then I would have been at her mercy. She might have wished me to do something I was not ready to do, thus guilt would have overcome me.

I was afraid if I had stopped to be with her some in our group would have looked strangely wondering what I was doing. Others might have become impatient saying, "This isn't the time or place for that". Therefore, I pulled my arm away leaving this poor woman stranded and taking away any hope she may have had. I was afraid to give myself. I let the others decide my direction. My faith was weak and my fear was strong. I gave her no hope.

Who of you pulls his arm away from someone in need? Do you let others direct your life even though you know God wishes something different for you and from you? Are you also afraid of criticism, group pressures, or do you think God will disadvantage you?

If we help, often we are afraid we will risk losing material wealth such as many nice clothes, a beautiful house, a fast car, or money. Nevertheless, God always blesses those who give. In addition, giving people are happy people. They have good feelings with no guilt.

No one can win without risk. Nothing was ever accomplished without risk. A proverb says, "It's better to have risked and failed than not to have risked at all." All progress involves risk. Risk often threatens or frightens us. We fear the unknown. Sören Kierkegaard, a Danish philosopher and theologian, once said man must "take the leap of faith". He must leap into the unknown; he must take a step beyond; he must go where he is unsure; and do that of which he is uncertain. He must trust his God even if he does not understand.

Our Christian duty is to risk that for what we believe is right, to "take the leap of faith", by giving to the underprivileged and helping the handicapped.

Jesus reached out his arms and accepted the crippled, wicked woman, forgiving and healing her. I pulled my arm away from the woman closing any likely contact we might have had. I failed to "take the leap of faith".

My hope is that we can free ourselves from our selfishness and risk ourselves for something God wishes. We can pray for God's guidance knowing he is right. If we do God's will, we will express our love, compassion, and forgiveness, to the deprived and disabled. My personal hope is that I can reply to God's desires by serving others.

For the past 10 years during my work on Palgum Island, I have donated time, energy, and money to this Medical/Mission Center. This has been my choice. We can all choose. There are many places in the world where help is desperately needed such as in South Africa where the Yang Dong Church is supporting a World Mission Center. This center will be built to include a church, a campus ministry hub, a school and some housing for the homeless.

We can ask God to lead our giving in supporting this project. Our goal should be to pray continually asking for God's guidance so we know where and how we should give. Any aid we can offer the sick and deprived in South Africa or anywhere is answering God's wish.

Each one of us can help somewhere. My hope for me is that I am able to give not only my arm but also my total self to the sick and underprivileged. This could also be your hope.

Jesus gave physical, mental and spiritual health to his folk. He did not wait for the masses to come to him. He went to them. This is also our Christian responsibility, to go to the people, to assist where we can, maybe in South Africa, or somewhere else in the world.

We Christians can go to the people and give ourselves as Jesus did. We might actually visit a country and physically help. Making money available is another aid. Donating our time or talents is also possible. Jesus' people had faith in him. We want the people of the world to have faith in us. Jesus refused no one even if some had different customs, religions, or cultures.

Christians have a big responsibility. How can we respond to our brothers and sisters in the world? Are you and I willing to risk and care for the sick, disadvantaged and destitute?

Prayer: Let us pray.

Dear Lord, we need to trust you and we need to risk for what we believe is right. This is one of the most difficult of all tasks, to love, forgive and accept a person as he or she is. Please guide us so we are able to aid the homeless, handicapped and underprivileged. Give us strength and courage allowing us to take this frightening "leap of faith", so we can support others, physically, mentally and spiritually. In the name of Jesus, who gave himself to all people, at all times and in every circumstance. AMEN

Congregational Direction:

Dear friends, Go out into the world, and be charitable.
Help, and give with love and compassion.
Serve humanity, as you know God desires.

Benediction: (Numbers 6: 24-26)

> May the Lord bless you and protect you. May the Lord's face shine on you, and be gracious to you. May the Lord favor you, and give you peace. Through Jesus Christ, Amen

Jesus as Prophet

Seong Nam, Shin Kwang Church, 11.15.2009

Advent Sermon

Text: Hebrews 1:1-3

1. Long ago God spoke in many different ways to our fathers through the prophets [in visions, dreams, and even face to face], telling them little by little about his plans.

2. But now in these days he has spoken to us through his Son, to whom he has given everything, and through whom he made the world and everything there is.

3. God's Son shines out with God's glory, and all that God's Son is and does marks him as God. He regulates the universe by the mighty power of his command. He is the one who died to cleanse us and clear our record of all sin, and then sat down in highest honor beside the great God of heaven.

Advent wreaths, Christmas trees, candles, Christmas cards, Christmas carols and presents; somewhere in the midst of all this is the person Jesus. No it is not Christmas, but in two weeks we celebrate the 1st of Advent, the coming of Jesus. If the church does not teach us about the person Jesus, who will? In the secular world, in the western world, Jesus often gets lost in our many worldly customs. The church wants to teach of God's coming in Jesus, but with sports events, business engagements, school activities, family gatherings, Thanksgiving dinners and Christmas parties, Jesus frequently gets lost. Maybe it is different in Korea, but I think here we also have to be careful about forgetting Jesus in the midst of all our activities.

Even though we often overlook Jesus no one can say, "Jesus of Nazareth means nothing to us". In the Presbyterian Shorter Catechism, a book of Christian teachings, we read, "Christ as our Redeemer executes the offices of prophet, priest and king in both humility and exaltation." Yes, Jesus executes the office of prophet.

On this Sunday I will talk about the prophet Jesus. We can begin to understand Jesus' personality as he performs his visionary life. Furthermore, Jesus replicates God in his highest glory and in the most overwhelming way imaginable. Jesus was not only the utmost prophet, priest and king; he is the Christ!

In our present world there are many prophets such as philosophers, psychics and maybe political figures. During Jesus' life a group of spiritual leaders in the Jewish public created the word "prophet". These prophets were preachers, teachers, poets, mystics, healers and at times governmental consultants, who were documented as being remarkably stimulated by the Holy Spirit. Prophets were frequently religious rebels. They did not hesitate to attack existing religious rites and practices in God's name. Prophets sometimes attacked kings and governments for their acts of inhumanity and injustice. They were fanatical when it came to God's virtue and judgment.

Prophets often foretold the griefs, which thoughtless, disbelieving, and self-virtuous countries would experience. Simultaneously, they would foresee ages, when God would rule in compassion over regretful and compliant nations. With the motto, "Thus says the Lord," they wanted their society to know God's demands for both his holiness and compassion.

Accordingly we can understand when many of Jesus' followers recognized he was prophetic. We read in Luke 9: 7 - 8: "When reports of Jesus' miracles reached Herod, the governor, he was worried and puzzled, for some were saying, 'This is John the Baptist come back to life again', and others, 'It is Elijah or some other ancient prophet risen from the dead.' These rumors were circulating all over the land." In John 4:9-20 we read the story of Jesus surprising the Samaritan woman at the well. She was amazed by his remarks about living water and his extraordinary insight into her private life. She said, "Sir, you must be a prophet." Also after feeding the crowd at the Sea of Galilee, we read in John 6:14, "When the people realized what a great miracle had happened, they exclaimed, 'Surely, he is the prophet we have been expecting'"!

Even today, it is not difficult for most people to recognize that Jesus was a prophet, a Hebrew spiritual advisor similar to Isaiah, Jeremiah, Amos and Micah, who had a profound ethical influence on all the nations. Jesus was considered for many Gentiles and Jews as the prophet from Nazareth. Many also recognized the prophetic expression, "Thus says the Lord." In all time periods prophets are those who speak for God and challenge us to pay attention. Often citizens in past eras puzzled about prophets. Also today we often wonder about astonishing prophetical claims made, and maybe we too refuse to heed them. Prophets are frequently like "voices crying in the wilderness;" no one hears them. Repeatedly, we merely hear, "Jesus is a past prophet of spiritual antiquity". Some take note and some do not.

Many do honor Jesus as a consecrated person, whose message is taken to the highest level by God and is exalted to the maximum height. However, in these modern times with our computers, miracle medicines, medical operations and with space travel, Jesus is often far from us. Some say God is not really essential for us today.

When we identify Jesus as a past prophet he can easily be forgotten. Thus, in our homes, neighborhoods, offices, schools and universities and in our political communities Jesus often passes by ignored.

A true prophetical person always deals with actual life. He relates to personal, social, economic and political affairs of the present and future. A prophet does not sit on a haughty summit giving his divine judgments to those who want to take heed.

Jesus was not separated from the life of his people but was living totally with his folk. He was a friend of everyone including the rich and the poor. He was wedged in throngs with the sick and the guilty. Jesus knew what it was like to be valued, but he was also starved, harassed, loathed and deceived, and during his life he was tortured.

Jesus was much more than only a completely fulfilled prophet. A normal prophet speaks for God and says, "Thus says the Lord". Many times Jesus quoted the Jewish law and the prophets, and then would say, "You have heard, it has been said", and then he ventured to say, "But I say unto you..."

Jesus professes his God and our God with something so credible and with such authority it is impossible to ignore him. It is easy to understand why Jesus generation said that no one has ever spoken like Jesus speaks. Somehow when Jesus speaks it is like God himself speaking to us. Jesus words and actions reproduce flawlessly his life. God was speaking through Jesus to his folk. Like no other prophet Jesus said what he lived, and lived what he said.

We need to reflect on this astonishing imprint, which Jesus left to all his people in order to help us recognize the meaning of Jesus today. We must contemplate about what it was that made people, like you and I, come to the conclusion that Jesus was much more than only a prophet.

We can say, "God is brought to us through spiritual prophets. Prophets make it conceivable for us to recognize God as a genuine, as an intimate, as a challenging, yet as a rescuing God, one who loves us unconditionally". The New Testament authors relate to us that Jesus brought God to them in a most astounding, entirely new, noticeably unique and in a completely overwhelming manner.

The apostles could not find words and images to express this amazing Jesus appropriately. God in Jesus was so holy that the Hebrews did not use his name. They referred to God as the Tetragrammaton, coming from the Greek word Tetragrammatos, meaning the four letters, "Y H W H", pronounced "Yahweh" in the Hebrew language.

In our Hebrew text, we read, "Long ago God spoke in many different ways to our fathers through the prophets...But now in these days he has spoken to us through his Son," God spoke through them in visions, dreams, and even face to face. In these last days Jesus also speaks to us. It is clear that God has also always spoken through a countless diversity of men and women.

Yes, God also spoke through his Son. The word "Son" here means; a personal being, which is in a faultless likeness to the one we call our "Heavenly Father". Of course this is Jesus, the Christ.

Have you ever had a "pen pal"? You get to know him often and differently through his letters and e-mails. But it is totally a different experience when you meet him personally. Now you learn about your "pen pal" on a special, close, private basis. You can begin to have a deeper friendship with him in a fresh manner. Learning about God through prophets is similar to learning about a person through "pen pals". Now in our world some people only know God as a "pen pal". Their knowledge of God through Prophets is indistinct, inadequate and objective. Jesus, on the other hand, brings us to God intimately, affectionately, disturbingly, but kindly. This is as if you meet your "pen pal" privately and warmly.

Jesus brings God personally close to us because of his amazing words and actions. Jesus said, "If you knew me, you would know my father as well." (John 8:19b). No prophet has ever used these words. Only Jesus said this, therefore we know Jesus is more than a prophet.

God is brought to us through biblical prophets, who speak to us in many words; robust and touching words, and words that alter lives. Additionally with the Advent of Christ, we read, "And Christ became a human being and lived here on earth among us and was full of loving forgiveness and truth." (John 1:14a). In this connection we often read, "The Word became flesh and dwelt among us."

In two weeks we celebrate the first week in Advent, Jesus' coming and his birth. The Word became flesh! God became Jesus and lives in our midst!

It often takes us much time to know Jesus is the "Word". The "Word", the person Jesus comes to us, into our world, into our lives, into our pleasures and griefs, into our burdens, and into our illnesses and bereavements, bringing us our Lord. We recognize Jesus now, as he comes to us, through the words and actions he left. We rejoice in his Advent, his approaching, when we triumph and think of his birth on Christmas Day. Yes, Jesus was much more than only a prophet! He is the Christ!

Prayer: Let us pray:

Dear God, give us a new vision of the Christ you sent to us. Let us draw closer to him. Let us know him in a fresh light. Let us serve him in a new, enthusiastic way. Let us experience the fact that he is much greater than only a prophet. He is the Messiah! In Jesus' Name, Amen.

Benediction: (Numbers 6: 24-26)

May the Lord bless you and protect you.
May the Lord's face shine on you and be gracious to you.

May the Lord favor you and give you peace forever.
Through Jesus, the Messiah, Amen

The Present to Nicodemus

Seong Nam, Shin Kwang Church, 23.12.2007

Christmas sermon

Many places in the Old Testament tell us of the Messianic prophecies. Our first reading is Isaiah 7:10-17.

Mary waited for her son's coming; we are waiting to celebrate his birth. Our second reading is Mathew 1:18-25.

The Christmas gift-giving-time is approaching, we read about God's gift to us. The third reading is Romans 6:23b, "the gift of God is eternal life in Jesus Christ our Lord".

Text: John 3:1-21

It was evening, and the moon was shining over Jerusalem. Nicodemus carefully snuck through the shadows in order to meet Jesus. He found Jesus and listened intently to his words. However, he did not expect such rich teachings from this simple, uneducated carpenter. Jesus must have truly loved Nicodemus. He gave Nicodemus his most important teachings, about the kingdom of God and the life he must lead in order to enter God's kingdom. During that unforgettable evening, Jesus offered him the gift of everlasting life. At this time, Nicodemus began openly to acknowledge his own belief. Thus, he defended Jesus, when Jesus confronted the Pharisees with their own failure to keep their set of laws. (John 7:50-51) In addition, after Jesus died, Nicodemus brought myrrh and aloes to his tomb. (John 19:39)

"'But how is it possible', asked Nicodemus, 'for a man to be born, when he is old? Can he enter his mother's womb a second time, and be born?'" He thought, "That's ridiculous; no one can be born twice".

Jesus was a patient teacher, but he was certainly surprised, and somewhat disappointed about his question, because Nicodemus himself was a Pharisee and a well-known, well-educated teacher. He should have known these things. Nicodemus and his colleagues, the other Pharisees, had of course also heard about being born again and about eternal life, but they never thought seriously about it.

Nicodemus was no longer young, and now he wanted the entire, final, and factual answers on this matter. We might ask the same question, "How can we be born twice?"

We have heard about a re-birth, and eternal life, but often we have not responded. Maybe we think these words have no real meaning for us today, even though they may sound good. Nicodemus thought similarly, but he had the ambition to learn more. This desire to learn more could also be a positive quality for us. Nicodemus believed that what Jesus taught was important, but he could not truly understand Jesus' teachings. Frequently neither do we comprehend. Nicodemus wanted the genuine facts, only from Jesus, because he sincerely believed Jesus had the truth. The truth is, "God loved the world so much, that he gave his only Son, that whoever believes in him shall not die, but have everlasting life". (John 3:16)

This will be my first Christmas in Korea, and I recognize Koreans and westerners do not celebrate Advent and Christmas exactly the same way. During the Advent season, we celebrate each Sunday before Christmas with a candle. Today is the fourth and last Sunday before Christmas. On this day, we rejoice with four Advent candles to prepare for Jesus' birthday, which we celebrate on December 25.

What does Christmas mean? In the western world, we look at the beautiful Christmas trees, with their shining stars, colorful Christmas balls, sparkling ornaments, candy canes, and other decorations. We all enjoy big turkey dinners and presents we give to each other from our rich, materialistic world. It is a beautiful, amazing time, but certainly not only because of the material temptations of Christmas gift exchanging. Christmas is a wonderful time because of the birthday we celebrate in two days. For many people, this is the most wonderful time of year. With our families, close friends, and maybe lonely people, we sit around the Christmas tree, reading about Jesus' birth, telling Christmas stories, and singing Christmas carols. I feel the special presence of God's Spirit.

God's gift to us was Jesus. He was given to us, so we could learn about re-birth, and eternal life. God sent Jesus, because he loved the world so much. God loves us, even more than we love our children. Even if our child does something so wrong, we forgive him in spite of his misdeed. God forgives us even more, for our inhuman actions.

God not only gave us Jesus. He offers us life, but not only earthly life. Through his love, and compassion, he gives us the possibility of attaining eternal life. He gives us not only a new life beyond this one; he offers us a new life now. How do we understand this new life, this re-birth, this eternal life? Our understanding should be different from Nicodemus. Re-birth or new life is more than just our physical birth here on earth. New life is being truly alive in a very special way in this life.

We are truly alive, when we experience fulfilling happiness, vivid joy, and inner peace, and when we have given love to those around us, or when the love of Jesus radiates from our faces, and our lives. Someone who has this spiritual radiation is recognized as a child of God, or someone living in God's light and in his presence. I am sure many of you have experienced such people, around Christmas or at other times, who radiate God's love.

Eternal life is in the present, because we can experience it now, even though earthly life has restrictions. Eternal life is also in the future, because we will experience it when we leave this world. Then we will exchange our human body for a spiritual body. Eternal life becomes complete and perfect, with both parts of life: with the truly spiritually alive person in this present life, and with the spiritual body in the future life.

God, through Jesus, has offered us the gift of new life. We can have new life without earning it, but there is a problem. A gift we need not earn; we are only required to accept it. The danger is the non-acceptance.

Our God is a jealous God. He wants us to experience his gift, and do his will. He wants us to accept his gift of love, his gift of the Holy Spirit and his gift of new life. He does not want to compete with the material world.

When our friends or families give us gifts, they also want us to accept them. Maybe we refuse a gift thinking, "Oh, I don't deserve this gift. I have enough of that stuff anyway. I don't need it." We can deeply hurt ones' feelings, if we refuse their gifts.

God's feelings get hurt too, if we do not accept what he offers us. Even Christians sometimes say, "God, I don't merit what you want to offer me". Even worse, "God, I have enough of you! I have more important things." Wow, how can a person say that! We always need what God wants to present us.

Certainly, if we know eternal life exists, how can we cast it off? If we reject God's offer, if we choose man's material world, if we go the lower road, instead of the higher road, saying "no" to God, then, we must realize, we alone convict ourselves; God does not convict us. We may realize our error of non-acceptance, when we are seldom happy, or cannot master our lives. Maybe we are constantly depressed, have no interest in participating, don't know what is missing in our lives, get angry for no reason, use alcohol, cigarettes, and other drugs, or we no longer enjoy friends and relatives. If this is our life, we punish, and convict ourselves. However, we can be happy, because God will help us! In verse 17, we read, "It was not to judge the world that God sent his Son into the world, but that through him the world might be saved".

When we are able to receive this re-birth, we consequently understand Christian faith as a child understands it. Nevertheless, how can we, as adults, practice a child-like Christian faith, thus experiencing re-birth? A small child trusts his parents unconditionally. Parents can tell him anything, and a child will believe them. Our goal as adults is similar, to believe without questions. This sounds rather naïve.

Jesus said, "Truly, I tell you, who ever does not accept the kingdom of God like a child will never enter it". (Mark 10:15) Do we have child-like faith? Faith means belief without proof. We cannot prove God, so we must have faith, in order to accept God's gift of new life. Without faith we cannot be born again, and experience new life!

Further, when we have faith, material temptations, such as Christmas gifts, do not exist. These gifts then, become part of our joyous, giving at Christmas.

One final question: Why can some people not accept God's gift? Why do some people live without belief? Unfortunately, some so-called devout Christians have made it impossible for struggling Christians and others to accept God's gift of new life. These distressed individuals have been disillusioned when experiencing unloving, intolerant, non-accepting, and judgmental deeds from these pious Christians.

Also in our academic world intellectuals might say, "Life without belief is not a mistake, but rather an honorable conclusion. Such people are honest, and stand by their convictions. Honest doubt is always better than hypocrisy."

This might be true, but I also think most people reject faith, not for intellectual reasons, but, because of selfish stubbornness. They want to see, hear, and understand what they desire, because they are afraid to live as Christians. They do not know what a true Christian life is. They would rather live in the shadows of Christianity, because they are afraid of what others might think, if they say, "I am a believing Christian". If they confess themselves as Christians, they may be afraid, they would lose perhaps their identity. Truly, with Christ, their identity would strengthen.

Maybe some are afraid to live in God's light as spiritual people, because spiritual people's lives are changed. They want no change; they are satisfied with their present lives. They do not know what to expect if they change their lives, if they become new people, born again people. Conversely, acknowledging God's gift of new life, people want to change; they want to live different and fulfilled lives. Then they will not lose in life's eternal game, but they will win and be happier people.

Will we be able to celebrate the birth of Jesus, in a new light, when Christmas is here, a day after tomorrow? Can we understand why Christmas and the birth of Jesus are so important for us? Sometimes it is difficult to comprehend! Jesus was born, so that we could lead and experience a new life, a life for others. God sent Jesus to us, so we could be born again. To be "born again" means to accept Jesus and his teachings. When we practice Jesus' teachings, we are able to live a more content, meaningful, worthwhile, and peaceful life. Yes, we can begin this new life now, here on earth.

Prayer: Let us pray.

Dear Lord, help us to understand the meaning of Jesus, and his birth. We not only want to talk the truth of your Gospel, but we also want to do the truth of your Good News. Then we can experience your promise of eternal life, new life, and re-birth. In Jesus' name, Amen.

Understanding the Easter Story

Pohang, Hana Church, April 19, 2006; Sang Nam, Shin Kwang Church, April 15.2007

Easter Sermon

Readings: I Corinthians 15; John 20:1-16

Text: John 20:24-29

"A week later his disciples were in the house again and Thomas was with them. Though the doors were locked, Jesus came, and stood among them, and said, 'Peace be unto you'."

Even though we celebrated Easter last Sunday, I still keep thinking about it. Sometimes I ask myself, if we truly understand the Easter story.

"Though the doors were locked, Jesus came, and stood among them". It was the physical Jesus, not an apparition, or a hallucination, but the living Jesus. Because he entered through the shut and locked doors, Jesus' followers were distressed and frightened. Now Thomas, one of the twelve apostles, could finally see Jesus and after putting his fingers into the nail marks in Jesus' hands and into his side, he became a believer. Though many of Jesus' disciples believed without his appearance after the Calvary crucifixion, their faith was very much strengthened.

This human Jesus was the man we read about in the Gospels, who ate and drank, joked and wept, and had expectations and doubts, as we do. They could touch this man, who was the authentic Jesus, who came into that room through bolted doors. Now we are confronted with the Resurrection miracle. It was the same Jesus, with whom they had navigated on the Sea of Galilee, slumbered in the fields around that lake, feasted with disreputable individuals and came perspiring down the dusty trails to Capernaum or one of the other villages in the area. Now his friends knew what they had sometimes sensed, that somehow this man was distinct and extraordinary. There was another element to this man they loved. His Resurrection had freed in him his holiness he had set aside at his crucifixion. He was no more a captive, in space and time, as are we. I have no idea what kind of body he had, since he could go through closed doors and yet anyone could feel the wound marks in his side. Was it a spiritual body? How is it possible to see a spiritual body and feel the wound marks? What kinds of people live in heaven? Are they spiritual or physical people or both? Then I repeat the Apostles' Creed, "I believe in the Resurrection of the body, and the life everlasting." It is unclear so we cannot answer this question.

Jesus' Resurrection is truthfully a miracle story, a happening entirely outside of our capability of comprehension. What actually happened on Easter morning two and a half days after he died? We cannot prove the Resurrection so we need to have faith in what occurred that Sunday. I have faith that in some miraculous way the glory was upon Jesus when he got to his feet. Life came into him again and he continued his Christly life. With great joy, I tell to you today, he has risen.

This story of Jesus, who lived, died, and rose is one of the most significant biblical stories and one of the paramount stories for the world. This Resurrection created a Church that persisted through centuries of persecutions, ridicule of the theorists, corruptions of its administrators and the foolishness of its supporters. This new church covered every part of this earth. Its message was, "Jesus our Lord is risen!" This story has formed the western world for more than two thousand years. No human event has yet to replace the Resurrection. This story is not only intended for the western world, but it is also important for all of us here in Korea. Most important is that this story is proving effective today as in the past. It grasps the thoughts and spirits of individuals like you and I. It calls us to renew our lives, which is nothing less than being "born again". (See my sermon "The Present to Nicodemus".) When this becomes your story and mine, life begins anew, rebirth occurs.

Nevertheless, how do you hear the story? There are ways to hear and ways to be deaf. Some people perceive the Resurrection with disbelief, as did the disciples at first. They rejected the women's story, when they came running to disciples, with the account of the vacant crypt. The apostles thought the women spoke nonsense, thus they did not believe them. Finally, the apostles became convinced except for Thomas. "Thomas was not with the rest, when Jesus came. So the disciples told him, 'We have seen the Lord.' Thomas said, 'Unless I see the nail marks in his hands, unless I put my fingers, where the nails were, and my hand into his side, I will not believe.'" In addition, some scholars ridiculed the idea about the resurrection of the dead.

The problem is not so much the ridicule and mocking of the Resurrection. It is the assumption this story cannot be true. It is the theory that miracles do not occur. Jesus was dead and he cannot be resurrected.

The Resurrection story is the triumphant confirmation of the Gospel, which has proven and is proving itself to be probably the greatest story ever told. Jesus still comes to us even if our doors are closed. Many of those, who have not listened to this Christian account, are now beginning to listen. Even though it is a miracle, the time comes when even mocking atheists are ready to listen again. This miracle is not explained or proven. It is experienced when faith takes the place of proof. Jesus comes again to you and me through our closed doors as he went through the closed doors at the Resurrection.

Probably today, people are less mocking sceptics but rather half-Christians. They desire to accept the Bible story and rejoice in a returning faith. When the churches show new dynamism, they rejoice. Nevertheless, they find themselves fluctuating between belief and non-belief.

Therefore, it is very tempting to settle for the figurative resurrection story. Such people might say, "The Resurrection means life is victory over death and hope is victory over despair. Hope is the truthful condition of our human spirit". It is wrong to disparage his way of understanding the Easter story. It is wrong to deprive the half-Christian of his Easter belief and joy. Some wonderful people of intellectual honesty could never say they do not believe some parts in Christianity.

The figurative Easter story was not what the apostles or the early Christians heard. It was not the belief that moved to all parts of the earth and it is generally not what brings a regeneration into our lives today. This regeneration is what we call "rebirth".

We should to be ready at any moment for the Spirit of Jesus to walk through our door and say, "Put your finger here; see my hands." Also, "Happy are they, who never saw me, and yet have found faith." It matters not, if we put our hands into Jesus' side or look at the scars in his hands, or if we have faith without seeing Jesus. What is important is that we are ready to be regenerated, to be reborn.

Then, of course, it is possible to hear the Easter story out of habit. We churchgoers are so often enclosed in the small area of sacred repetition. The doors are closed, not because of non-belief, or half-belief, but because of every day monotony. This routine is probably the most challenging door for us to go through.

Jesus also had a religious routine. It was his custom to attend every Sabbath in the synagogue. The people he found most difficult to touch were not the cynics, the half-believers, or the ridiculers, but the believers, who were so covered with ordinary beliefs of monotony that they could not enter life's spirit of spontaneity.

Do you hear the Easter story with minds alert to what is being reported by eyewitnesses and with minds open to the possibility that this was no ancient legend, but the supreme miracle? I hope we hear with life's spirit of freedom, ready to respond to the Easter event. We want Easter to come to us, not only in our thoughts, but also through the splendid confirmation of believing hymns and sounding trumpets. Hopefully, this will help us respond to the Easter story and live as Jesus did. I hope we realize, we are not alone, but surrounded by the living Church in every land. I hope we hear all nations responding to our whisper of "He has risen. Hallelujah! He has risen indeed."

"Though the doors were locked, Jesus came, and stood among them"; the real Jesus came. You can unlock your doors now. You can open them wide for him today. The spirit of Jesus can come to you and be with you right now. His spirit can speak to you this very moment. You can enter God's Kingdom this very Sunday. May his spirit be with all of you so you are able to open your doors. He wants to guide your lives. Amen.

Prayer: Let us pray.

Dear Lord, let us open our doors to you now in this church service. We want to feel your presence. We want to feel the Easter joy. Let your Holy Spirit come into our lives at this time. Let us know the true meaning of the Easter message. We ask this in the name of Jesus the Christ, who was truly resurrected after his crucifixion on the cross. We ask this in the name of Jesus the Christ, who came to help us in this world and free us from all our wrong doings. We ask this in the name of Jesus the Christ, Amen.

Benediction:

> May the Lord bless you and keep you,
> May the Lord let his face shine upon you,
> and be gracious unto you,
> May the Lord lift up his countenance upon you,
> and give you peace until we meet again.
> In the name of Jesus Christ our Lord. Amen.

Witnessing

Seong Nam, Shin Kwang Church, 17.10.2010; Dubai, Kwanglim Church, 19.11.2010

Pentecost season

Reading: Acts 4: 13-31

Scripture: Acts 1:1-8

Our text today is Acts 1:8: "But you shall receive power, when the Holy Spirit has come upon you; and you shall be my witnesses in Jerusalem, and in all Judea and Samaria and to the end of the earth".

This is an extraordinary promise made to a group of twelve typical citizens chosen almost at random. In this inexplicit corner of the Roman Empire, they were all members of an oppressed and disheartened state. Yet, this dismayed folk did receive power. It was not military, economic, or political power. It was the kind of power, which did not lead to corruption or disaster. This nation and today's world are hungering for that power which was to come. It was the moral and spiritual power, which changes defeated and hopeless lives. It enabled people to be honorable, love mercy, and walk humbly with their God. It was the power of God's Spirit, which totally possessed Jesus of Nazareth. It empowered Jesus to bring forgiveness to the guilty, to heal the sick in mind and body, to cast out evil spirits, and to liberate the enslaved. It was the promise that Jesus gave his disciples: "You shall receive power, when the Holy Spirit has come upon you."

On that Pentecost day, Luke expressed in the Acts' story the coming power. With symbols of wind and fire, he tells us what a number of everyday people experienced. They were apathetic and disordered followers of Jesus, who would be given an unknown power from an unknown source, which Jesus called "the Kingdom of God". An unbiased spectator might have dismissed the incident as another example of the euphoric mystical outbreaks, which were as common in those days as today. Some of the onlookers thought the disciples were intoxicated. Peter told them the bars were not yet open that early in the day. Their inebriation was from the power of God's Spirit. It was a divine passion meaning that God was with them. What they were experiencing was not some fleeting pious fury, but a compulsion to pass on to others the spiritual and moral power they had found in Jesus. They had no other ambition except to tell the story of his life, death, and resurrection, and to demonstrate his power to liberate and renew.

Not only did the Spirit come to these people but also the rest of the promise came true: "You shall be my witnesses in Jerusalem". The apostles told of Jesus' resurrection in Jerusalem, where he had been crucified. They were witnesses in all of Judea. This new movement then spread rapidly across to the land of Samaria, an enemy province. It crossed these barriers of ethnic and religious variances and to all parts of the earth. Today we call this crusade Christianity. Yes, you and I sitting here today in our Korean church are living witnesses that the story of Jesus sped across the centuries bringing the Good News to the entire human race. Here is one of the most amazing historical accounts we have. From that tiny cluster of people in Jerusalem, the Gospel grew spreading over the entire globe.

Dispersing the Good News was accomplished through witnessing and testifying to Jesus. It spread by word of mouth and many actions through the power of the Holy Spirit. The witnessing was not accomplished by the brilliance or prestige of the disciples. They were not particularly brilliant or significant people. Witnessing and spreading the Good News was not accomplished only by a series of charismatic leaders like Peter, Paul and their successors. Witnessing was not accomplished by strong supportive and efficient organizations. The Good News was spread by the power of the Spirit and was conveyed by ordinary men and women who lived by the Spirit of Jesus and were glad to tell others about him. In other words, this new Christianity was both real and infectious. All who were yearning for a life with significance, worth, and ethical integrity were drawn to these men and women, who possessed the Holy Spirit.

These first Christians did not squeeze their faith and witnessing into a small container and keep it hidden. They did not keep it apart from their family life, or exclude it from their occupation or their opinions and their interaction with others. Their religion was central and was the key to their whole personality. Their discussions, actions and Christian convictions were always considered. It was in their nature to routinely witness for Christ and Christianity. The authorities told Peter and John to stop talking about Jesus. They said however, "We can only speak the things, which we have seen and heard." They could not have ignored Christianity. Christianity was not merely something private but it concerned all people.

Sometimes we think a person's religion means little to him when we consider his character or when his beliefs are no more important than the type of toupee he wears or his enthusiasm for baseball, soccer, or golf. If we think he only occasionally follows religious tradition because of ritual, for example going to church, this, his religious indifference could be true. If, on the other hand, true Christianity means total commitment, of which the Bible speaks, then his character in not that of a genuine Christian. Often we only see part of a person's personality. Judging one is very dangerous and something we should not do.

We must be aware spiritual commitment determines our attitudes, shapes our opinions, and guides all our decisions every day, both private and public. Our deepest beliefs, Christian or not, create our character, our goals in life, and our words and actions. Wherever we are at home, on the job, in school, in social activities, or in casual conversations, we are witnessing our most profound faith. If we are believers, we witness as believers.

Jesus told his disciples and tells all of us who want to be his disciples today, "You are my witnesses". We are all his witnesses when we share in his mission now in this church and elsewhere. We are his witnesses in Korea and in the entire world when we minister to others. I come from another part of the earth and I pray I am a good witness for Christ here in this Korean church. In our daily lives, we are all his witnesses in every word we say and every action we take. Our deeds and behavior reflect the Spirit of Christ. If our religion is true, it will be of special public interest and value, and will show our Christianity.

In Acts Ch. 4: 13 – 31, we read about Peter and John being warned by the authorities not to witness to Jesus' healings and Resurrection. The authorities knew in their hearts Jesus was innocent and Peter and John had broken no laws. They knew they could not punish these men because of their witnessing. Thus, their religion became of special interest and value to the public.

Is my life or your life a reflection of the Spirit of Christ? Is my personal religion or is your personal religion of special public interest and value? Does the public recognize that the Spirit of Christ lives within me and within you?

Some people might protest saying, "Do you want us to support Christians, who speak publicly in loud trumpeting voices and in inapt manners? Do you want Christians to bring religion into every conversation and to all community events? Do you expect us to bring religion into every life situation to advertise our Christian convictions everywhere in the world and to force our values down the throats of our friends and colleagues?"

Paul would not have approved these acts and Jesus despised arrogant piety. Jesus said, "When you give alms, sound no trumpet before you, as hypocrites do, in the synagogues and in the streets, so they may be praised by men. Truly I say to you... when you give alms, your giving must be secret and your father who sees all that is done in secret will reward you; ...and when you pray, you must not pray like the hypocrites; for they love to stand and pray in the synagogues and on the street corners so they may be seen by men. Truly I say to you, they have had their reward. But when you pray, go into a room by yourself and pray to your father in secret. Your father sees what is done in secret and will reward you (spiritually)." (Mt. 6: 2-6) Using religion to show off to further one's personal career, to promote a private ambition is not what the Bible teaches. Further, that was not the disciples' witness of Jesus. Their witness was the natural, genuine, spontaneous reflection of their Christian spirit and evidence of their deepest beliefs.

The disciples were not told: "Go and announce to everyone what good Christians you are and force your opinions on them at every opportunity". Instead they were gently informed, "you shall receive power, when the Holy Spirit has come upon you and you shall be my witnesses... (v. 7)" All Christian witness which is arrogant and self-centered is false witness. For example, "I will go to church so people will see I am a good Christian." Or "I will put more money into the offering plate because someone is watching me; now I get the congregation's approval." Nevertheless, does God give his approval?

The only true witness comes naturally from the believer, who has received the power of the Holy Spirit. If we lack the Holy Spirit, our religion cannot interest and be of value to others. Therefore, we can only give little or no witness to Jesus Christ. Maybe we try desperately to devise ways of demonstrating our convictions, but if we lack the authority of the Holy Spirit, we are unable to convince others of our belief.

I think, however, many of us are guilty of being silent concerning our Christian convictions, rather than being loud and showy in our witness to the Lord!

In true Christianity, it is not your exterior which counts, but rather what is inside you that is important. If someone bumps into you or attracts your attention, what do they see in you? Do they see anger, self-pity, pride, arrogance, or something similar? On the other hand, do they see the inspiration of the Holy Spirit, the gift Christ has promised, which is imbedded deep inside us, which transforms our lives? Do they see our love, concern, understanding, and compassion? We receive the gift of the Holy Spirit through faith and prayer and it is nurtured in the community of Christ's church, which is everywhere including our Korean church here. Yes, we can be loud and showy in a quiet and humble way!

We might ask ourselves what we know about this inward power of the Spirit that can make us true and joyful witnesses to Christ. Without the power of the Holy Spirit we make poor witnesses and we are unwilling or unable to share the Good News of the Bible with others.

We are witnesses for the Christian church when we have bazaars, music programs, and other projects in our church. Churches throughout the world witness in the same way. Sometimes we witness for Christ by telling others our personal stories. We do so not to show-off our belief in public but in obedience to Jesus, who said, "You will be my witnesses", through the power of his Holy Spirit not through your physical strength. However, even more important is the Christian authority people see in our daily lives. With the Holy Spirit working in us, we can influence others in a Christian way, quietly but distinctly!

People will see Christianity is our central issue and will observe it through our deeds.

Prayer:

Dear lord, help us to witness for you not in a loud, boastful way as do the hypocrites. Let your Spirit work in us so people can see we are of God, that we have love, compassion, understanding, and forgiveness for others. We want to show our Christianity in a quiet modest way, not in an arrogant way, as do the heathens. Be with us now until we meet again. In Jesus' name, Amen.

Benediction: Ps. 67:1-2:

> God be gracious to us and bless us.
> Let your face shine upon us
> so that your ways may be known on earth.
> Let your saving power be known among all nations. AMEN.

"Who the Holy Spirit Is and How He Works"

Seong Nam, Shin Kwang Church, 27.05.2007

Readings: Joel 2:28-32; Acts 2:1-4

Text: John 16:7, 12-15

Pentecost

Today almost 2000 years ago, the Holy Spirit was poured out on about 3000 people resulting in the beginning of the Christian church (Acts 2:40). Today we are celebrating Pentecost Sunday. In my sermon I will talk about who the Holy Spirit is, how he worked in the lives of the early Christians and how he can work in our lives. Also the bond linking the Holy Spirit to the Trinity will be discussed.

John 16:7 says, "...I tell you the truth; it is for your good, that I am leaving you. If I do not go, your Helper will not come, but if I go, I will send him to you."

What Jesus left his disciples was not a memory, not a book, not a ritual, but the Holy Spirit, the Counselor, Comforter, Helper, and Advocate. The Bible tells us it will be advantageous for his disciples when Jesus physically leaves them. Only then will they experience his new divine presence of power. Further documentation of the coming of the Spirit is found in the Book of Acts and in the four Gospels. In Matthew, Mark, Luke and John there are many references to the presence of the Holy Spirit in the early Church. Previous biblical passages to the Spirit are relatively few. Something happened to the first Christians that made them aware Jesus was speaking to them. They began to bind themselves together in spite of all their differences. They set themselves free from the burdens of the traditional Jewish religion. They kept their minds opened for new truths. All this gave their lives new directions. The Spirit of Jesus, God's Spirit, the Holy Spirit, was now working in their lives. At this time, we begin to recognize the working of the Trinity.

We can search the Scriptures and not find a single passage that describes exactly who this Holy Spirit is. They describe what he does and most important what the results are of his doings. They tell us of their experience with the Spirit but not of the philosophies of the Spirit. The question remains: "Who is this Holy Spirit and how is he related to God, the Father and to Jesus, the Son and Christ?"

The words "God the Father" convey some kind of picture to us even though it is insufficient. The words "God the Son" suggest a specific image of Jesus in the Gospels. The words "God the Holy Spirit" describe absolutely no picture we can fathom. We find it impossible to make any kind of mental description of the Holy Spirit.

This non-visual, unexplainable representation of the Holy Spirit creates a problem for us if we are determined to have a logical, concrete, tangible and permanent vision of God. It presents a problem for us if we want Christianity and the Trinity to be a sequence of proposals which we can explain and prove. If on the other hand we want to find a God who is alive, active within us and in our world, and if we are seeking a belief that it is an experience of God's presence and power, then the Holy Spirit is our answer.

Think for a moment about two people, Han-wan and Yeong-mi, who are deeply in love. There are three elements in this situation: Han-wan, Yeong-mi, and the love that binds them. You could give some sort of description to Han-wan and to Yeong-mi, but how do you describe this mysterious something that flows between them? This mysterious something is real and very significant. It determines a great deal of what Yeong-mi and Han-wan say and do. However, just what is love?

Further, suppose you are at a concert completely involved in a great passage of music. Again, here are three essentials in this situation: you, the orchestra, and the magic bonding music, which gives you a feeling of bliss. The orchestra can be analyzed; you can be analyzed; but how do you analyze this mysterious involvement between you and the music?

Jesus compared the Holy Spirit to the Greek word "pneuma", wind, which "blows where it wills; you hear its sound, but you don't know from where it is coming, or to where it is going" (John 3: 8). You can't see the wind; you can't catch the wind; but you know it exists. You see and feel its effects, as the leaves rustle, as the sand whirls, as the grasslands are blown and as your face senses the breeze.

So on Pentecost we celebrate the Spirit, not by trying to explain his mystery, but by rejoicing in the signs of his activity in the secular world, in the Christian Church and in our own lives. In John 16, 13-15 Jesus speaks of the Holy Spirit as the one who does not draw attention to himself but is the Mediator, who reveals and illuminates the Christ and God. We read "The Spirit will guide you into all the truth; for he will not speak on his own authority, but will tell only what he hears (from God). He will make known to you the things which are coming. He will glorify me (Jesus); for everything he makes known to you, he will draw from what is mine. All that belongs to the Father is mine. That is why I said the Spirit will take from what is mine and make it known to you." The Holy Spirit reveals and illuminates God, the Father and Creator. He reveals and illuminates Jesus, the Son and the distinctive Christ properties in Jesus.

Jesus, the Christ, was entirely filled with the Holy Spirit from his birth to his crucifixion. He was overwhelmed, guided, and endowed by the Holy Spirit when he said on the Cross, "Father, into your hands I commit my spirit". As Jesus died on the cross, he gave his Spirit to the Father, so it could be emptied onto this new Christian body. What occurred on Pentecost, almost 2000 years ago, was the coming of Jesus' Spirit to empower that new community of Christians, to reveal God's love and to ensure his works. Pentecost was the beginning of the Christian church and the beginning of the working of the Trinity.

Most of us want a stronger faith, but since we disagree with some things in the organized church our belief falters. We differ with certain church guidelines and principles, or with the acceptance of certain church doctrines and declarations. The church of the New Testament on the other hand found that these officers, assemblies, and minor regulations were necessary and did not weaken their faith. Maybe the biggest difference between them and us is that they believed, in a deeper sense, in the renovating and energizing power of the Holy Spirit. Though most of us have the same goal as the early Christians it is often difficult for us to actualize these objectives since a great majority of us are generally more materialistic and are not able to understand the mystical. Maybe as Koreans it is easier for you to be more receptive to the mystical because of your shamanistic heritage.

I believe the western church is rediscovering unity in its organization. There was a time when in the United States and Europe, many Christian denominations would aggressively maintain that only their system of Church government was taught clearly in the New Testament. Currently many scholars agree it is impossible from today's texts to receive clear guidance on church government.

We here in Korea can also learn from various Korean and Western scholars, who belong to other Christian denominations. Certainly not only one church has all the answers. Other churches indeed also have good systems, ideas and solutions.

Sometimes today this problem of church differences causes congregation members to leave the church. In some cases new churches are formed as sometimes we observe here in Korea. This is certainly not always necessary. It should be possible to discuss differences and make some changes if truly needed. It may not be essential or not be possible to make all changes some think are necessary. In any case, though it takes strength and courage, honesty and diplomacy, openness and acceptance, we should be able to learn from each other, worship together in the same church with our differences and still keep our faith. We do not want to be restricted to our own limited knowledge and resources. We can broaden the minds of our incomplete selves with the awareness and viewpoints of others. As Christians we all have basically the same belief; that belief is the understanding and faith in the Trinity.

God's Holy Spirit flows freely surging anywhere he desires. We have to be open at all times if we want to experience his power. Yes, the early churches were organized but they were receptive to the ruling power of the Holy Spirit. Those who turned away from the organized church did not want to destroy their structures but rather to rebuild them using the reviving power of the Holy Spirit. Thus, our churches can also be both more human and more spiritual.

The Holy Spirit is here and now! Do you feel him? Have you felt him? He moves everywhere revealing to us the Father and the Son. He speaks through the truth wherever he is found. He brings to life our dead spirituality and brings new hopes and aspirations. He brings together individuals to form a true congregation in Christ. We therefore become not less but more genuine individuals and not less but more convinced Christians that "He is the Way, the Truth, and the Life" (John 14:6). AMEN.

Prayer:

O God, we pray that we may understand more about you so we may live our lives in the light of your Spirit. Let us be receptive when your Spirit speaks to us so we may do your will. Let us trust your Spirit so we can help those near us. Let us follow your Spirit so we can be fully enlightened. Lord, bless us now and forever. Be with us always especially on this Pentecost Sunday. In Jesus' name, Amen.

Hearing and Understanding the Holy Spirit

Seong Nam, Shin Kwang Church, 21.10.2007

Text: I. Corinthians 2:10-16

In the New Testament, we find many texts about what the Holy Spirit has done, and the results of his doings. However, it is difficult to find a satisfactory text which tells us practically how we can hear and understand the Holy Spirit. Therefore, today I will attempt to answer the following questions: "How can we hear and know the Holy Spirit, and how can he be part of us, so we can experience his power and recognize his working in our lives?"

These questions cannot be answered easily. For the Holy Spirit works in strange ways and his answers will always be different from what we expect. The Holy Spirit speaks even to those who do not want to listen to him. He speaks to all of us. However he rarely speaks to us in the same way and probably not verbally, but it is also possible to hear spoken words from him.

For example, Jesus' Holy Spirit spoke to the atheist Saul, who became Paul the Apostle. Saul was struck by a blinding light and was unable to see for 3 days. He could only hear Jesus' voice. Then, because Jesus convinced him there was more to life than just advancing his own career, Paul changed completely. Instead of persecuting Jesus and the new Christians, he fought fiercely for the causes of Jesus. (Acts 9, 1-31)

If we want to talk with God the Holy Spirit, hear and understand him, there are five vital rules we must follow. First, we need to "humble" ourselves. The more humble we are the easier it is to hear and know the Holy Spirit.

Second, we need to be "honest" with God. He knows better than we do if we are truthful to him. We may think we are being honest but maybe subconsciously we are trying to hide something from God and ourselves, thus being unaware of our dishonesty. Giving a church donation is good but if we think even unknowingly "Yes, this will also profit me" then we are being dishonest. The more honest we are with God the easier it is to hear and understand the Holy Spirit.

The third and fourth rules are to practice the Latin phrase "Ora et Labora", pray and work. We must sincerely be doing what we think God wants us to do. It is necessary for us to do everything possible in order to accomplish our goal. Simultaneously we need to bring our concern to God the Holy Spirit in prayer. Prayer is vital in communicating with the Holy Spirit. Therefore, it is essential to learn how to pray. Without prayer, it is impossible to truly hear and know the Holy Spirit.

"Ora et Labora" means pray and work. If we have not studied hard for an exam, we cannot expect to pass it by merely praying, "God, make me smart so I can pass". However, if we have studied hard we can pray, "Please God help me to relax and not be nervous during the exam. Help me to be able to answer the questions with all the knowledge I have learned." At the same time, remember we must be humble and honest with God.

The fifth rule is to be "receptive". It is important to be continually open to the Holy Spirit so we can recognize and understand the Spirit's voice. The Spirit may not communicate with us when we are listening or when we desire his help. We can hear the Spirit's voice through prayer and meditation. Praying for openness, understanding and direction is not always easy when we want to hear him. However all miracles are possible through prayer and all of us can experience the miracle of the Holy Spirit.

In order for us to experience the Holy Spirit's miracle, prayer needs to be part of our lives. We can use any language or dialect, speak politely, or impolitely, use good or bad language, pray aloud or silently, and the Spirit will listen and understand us. He does not think more or less of us by the way we pray but he will only recognize us and reply if we have followed the five rules. When we have complied with these five conditions, we can speak to God the Holy Spirit any way we wish knowing we will get an answer but we will not know when or how our answer will come or what his reply will be.

Now I have given you all the rules in order to hear, understand, and experience the working of the Holy Spirit. Nevertheless, the Holy Spirit will also speak in other ways! He may force people to listen to him. He may compel certain individuals to perceive his voice to know his wishes and to do his will.

Such individuals are those who do not want to listen for him and do not want to listen to him or who even fight violently against him, as did Saul. When God forces these people to recognize his will, they either have the choice of listening, grasping, and following his will, or not. Since they know his will, they must follow it if they do not want to be damned, as Jonah was in the Old Testament and as I was. Thank God, we both changed. Yes, we may follow all the rules to hear, understand and experience, but God's Spirit may speak to us in yet different ways!

Often we hear the Spirit but we do not understand him, as I experienced. For about 15 years, I heard the Spirit's voice calling but I ignored him because I did not truly understand. In any case, I did not want to become a minister, which I believed was my calling. Even though my life depended on his clarification, I wanted even more information in order to be completely convinced of what my goal should be. Because I did not get a satisfying answer from him, I gave God an ultimatum. I told him if He did not give me clarification now I would not go into the ministry and do his will. It took me a long time to understand what he was trying to tell me. In my ultimatum, I told God if he wanted me to understand he would have to hit me hard on the head. Yes, he hit me very hard, not physically but spiritually. Consequently, I finally heard, accepted, and began doing his will. Then a change began in my life. I was not entirely sure if God wanted me to alter my life, but he forced a transformation in me and I am very happy about the changes that began. This part of my life you will hear in my third story on the Holy Spirit.

I know it is not always easy to do God's will. We generally want to do what we want to do when we want to do it! That is normal and human.

Sometimes we really want to do God's will but we do not know what he wants us to do. We may even pray very seriously and still be unsure of his will. We want the Holy Spirit to answer our prayers but maybe we do not receive the answer we desire. We want a "YES" and we get a "NO". Therefore, we say, "God didn't answer my prayer". Moreover, because we think he did not respond, we say, "I knew there was no God, because if there was a God, he would have replied a 'YES'. Because of the 'NO' I cannot believe"!

However, are we sure God did not answer our prayer? The Holy Spirit may say "NO" or he may not reply until we are on our deathbeds. Maybe then we will hear, understand and follow. Because God speaks when he wishes, we must continually listen for his voice and then respond positively to him if we truly want to do his will and experience his power. This is often very difficult and at times may seem impossible to do his wishes! Thus if we give up trying to do what he desires for us, we truly will lose.

Here is another story. On this day, my prayers were extremely serious. I knew God wanted me to become a minister and I was sure I was doing his will by continuing my education.

Monday I was to begin my new work at Covenant Presbyterian Church in Palo Alto, California about 30 miles south of San Francisco. It was already Friday and I still had not found an apartment in which to live during my studies. I had looked all Friday morning and half of the afternoon but had had no luck. Now I was getting desperate. I truly did not know what more to do. Then I had an idea, "I could pray"! You know how it is when everything goes well for you, why should you pray. Because I knew I was doing God's will and because I had done all I could do to find an apartment, I could pray as I did. I prayed almost a little angrily, scolding God some too.

I prayed: "God, why don't you let me find an apartment? You know I have tried all day in vain. What is the matter with you? You want me to become a pastor but you will not let me find an apartment. You know I need one by Monday. What shall I do? I have done all I can do. Now it's up to you; you have to get me an apartment!" I gave God an ultimatum. I said, "If you don't want me to get this Master's degree, just don't let me find an apartment and I won't start my studies Monday!"

I prayed to God this way for about five minutes. I really did not know what else to do. I knew if I just sat there, nothing would happen, so I turned on the car ignition, drove around the corner, saw more apartments and drove to them.

I needed an apartment close to the church, not too expensive (I was a student), and one with large windows and suitable lighting conditions for good study.

I went to the manager's office and he opened the door. As I expected he said, "Sorry we have no vacancy". As I walked back to my car, while opening the door the manager called me back. "Just a minute, I might have a vacancy. A young Japanese woman should move out soon, but I have not seen her for several days. Maybe she has gone." He got the passkey and opened the door. Yes, she had left. The manager said I could move in the next day after they cleaned the apartment and changed the lock. I was shocked that God answered my prayer so fast and let me find the perfect apartment for my studies. "Ora et Labora!" Yes, I did pray and work!

God answered my prayer with a "YES" and he will answer your prayers too. I know he will. However, if God answers "NO" and if you truly want to do his will you must accept this answer! Since then I have received many "NO" answers, but also "YES" answers. On that occasion, I received a "YES" because God wanted me to continue studying to become a minister.

I do not know what answer you will get, but you will also get an answer. Remember, you must listen for God's voice constantly. He will communicate with you when he wants to speak. We even have to listen when we are not expecting an answer or do not need one. This is why it is extremely important to have daily prayer and meditation so we can hear when he gives us an answer.

Furthermore, God speaks to everyone differently. He speaks through the Bible, but also through other literature. He speaks through the past, present, and even the future. He speaks through illnesses, broken bones, and other accidents. He speaks through friends, enemies, and many experiences. One time God even spoke to me when I pricked my finger with a pin. How does God speak to you and how do you answer him?

Here is a final exceedingly important fact: When you truly do God's will, you will be very happy, incredibly satisfied, and extremely joyful! This is the truth.

Prayer:

O Lord, please be with all of us at this time, and in the future. Direct our lives. Let us hear your voice. Let us understand. Let us feel the presence, and power, of your Holy Spirit. Let us to do your will. In Jesus' name, Amen.

Benediction:

> May God, our creator,
> May Jesus, our example,
> May the Holy Spirit, our helper,
> Guide us and give us peace now and forever.
> In the name of our triune God,
> who loves us unconditionally, Amen.

Experiencing the Holy Spirit: No Other Choice

Seong Nam, Shin Kwang Church, 25.5.2008; Dubai, Han-In Korean First Church, 16.11.2012

Text: Jonah 1:1 – 3:3a

Last week we celebrated Pentecost, the coming of the Holy Spirit, and the beginning of the Christian Church. Therefore, today I will deliver my third sermon on the Holy Spirit. Its working in me made me realize why I had to become a pastor. It is essential to be aware that the Holy Spirit leads your life, as he led and leads mine.

Actually, I did not want to become a minister. Truly not, but I had no other choice.

During my summer vacations while attending the university, I worked in the wilderness of Alaska for the Alaska Dept. of Fish and Game. This was fascinating work, which still interests me greatly. At that time, I only wanted to be a biologist.

During the summer of 1965, I worked in Palmer, Alaska, about 50 miles north of my home in Anchorage. I had a very interesting job, which flew me over about 1200 square miles with a Fish and Game pilot. With a small plane and my pilot, I studied the vegetation habitat of the moose. In addition, I observed various undergrowth types and using aerial photos delineated these flora varieties onto topographic maps. Additionally, extensive foliage notations were made by plane, car and on foot. This was a summer of tremendously stimulating ecological employment.

One day my supervisor Joe, said, "We have a new area to examine". He showed me on a map where we had to go. He added that the well-known area west of Big Lake was not necessary to study. However, that was my target, since my father owned some property there and I was interested in developing this land someday.

The next day I drove directly to Crooked Lake, where our property was, even though Joe told me definitely not to go there! I was thoroughly enjoying this excursion and the beautiful scenery, not paying attention to where I was driving. At 11 AM, as I was arriving at my destination, the road began narrowing drastically. Consequently, I had to find a place to turn around. As I commenced turning, my situation became more problematic. I tried everything possible to head in the opposite direction, but all my efforts were in vain. Nearly 4 hours later, I was unable to improve my position.

There was a swamp on the left side of this small roadway and a steep ridge on the right side. Unfortunately, while I was trying to turn my vehicle, it lodged between two trees, one tree in front of my vehicle, and one on its right side. My panel truck was now perpendicular to the narrow road and half way up the bank. I tried jacking up the truck and pushing it off to the left but only got into a more precarious predicament.

Now I was desperate! "Don't drive there", I remembered Joe saying. In those days, there were almost no inhabitants in this area. About 10 miles away was another narrow road, but hardly used by anyone. This joyride was costing money, and it would cost more, if I left my vehicle there. Thus, I began to walk out, and if possible hitchhike to Palmer, but thumbing a ride was very unlikely with seldom a car driving this road. It was too far to walk. What was I to do? My hope was to arrive in Palmer by days end, and hope that Joe would not be very angry. It all seemed impossible!

About 100 feet down that trail I stopped, and said to myself, "No, I can't leave this car here. I certainly cannot!"

On that fateful afternoon as I was walking back to the car, I had a flash back of when I was five years old. I said, "When I get big, I want to become a minister". On Sundays in church, I always admired the minister standing high in the pulpit. He was very impressive to me as a five-year-old, with his deep voice and broad stature. Generally, little boys say they want to become police officers, firefighters, soldiers, doctors, or something similar, however definitely not ministers. Soon I forgot my wish until I was 14 or 15, when I felt I should become a minister. Nevertheless, I told no one my thinking except my mother, because I did not want my friends to think I was a pious goodie, goodie. In school, I prepared myself for the university. There I studied biology. During this time, I truly did not want to become a pastor, however secretly I knew I should. Was this to be my destiny? As time would tell, I had no other choice!

Back to my story: I knew I could not leave my panel truck on this road, so I did what I detested, despised, and what was selfish, but also human. Jonah did it, and probably most of us, when we are in very difficult situations. We have all most likely said, at one time or another, to God, or someone else, "If you do this for me, I will do that for you". Jonah said to God, "If you let me out of the fish's belly, then I will go to Nineveh, as you wish, and preach the Gospel". I said, "Okay God, if you want me to become a pastor I will, but only with one condition, only if you let me drive out of here within one hour". I made a deal with God!

I continued trying to free my vehicle, but could not drive forward and now it was impossible to drive backwards! Oh yes, I could back out into the swamp and then try to turn. Of course, I knew then what would have happened! I honestly could not imagine what to do, so I just aimlessly walked forward on this very narrow path thinking and looking for some answer, which I could not expect. I walked slowly about 25 feet down this trail thinking, and half praying, when suddenly a miracle happened! I found a log, eight-inches in diameter, which had been split lengthwise and was about six feet long. I could not fathom how exactly this log could have gotten there. It was the only timber in the vicinity and cut precisely the way I needed. I took the two halves and placed them into the swamp behind the rear wheels, then said a short prayer, and hoped the wheels would not slip off the planks as I slowly backed the panel truck onto them and into the swamp. Now I was in the middle of the swamp with my rear tires on those two slats. Gingerly, I shifted into forward gear as not to cause a jerking movement, resulting in the wheels slipping from the slats into the swamp — so far so good! I was almost holding my breath, when suddenly something slipped and then stopped! Wow, there was no plan B for me if the tires slipped off those split timbers. Then I drove slowly once again onto solid ground without incident! How lucky I was. Not one hour later, but 10 minutes later, I drove away. Yes, I made a big promise. I said I would become a minister, which was definitely not my goal. Was some entity trying to communicate with me by placing that wood exactly where I could use it? Was this a coincidence?

That afternoon, Joe had two flat tires while he was driving home from his fieldwork! How often does someone have one flat tire, not to speak of two? Joe waited and waited for me to drive by at about 6 PM so I could help him. When I finally drove by at 9 PM, he was gone. The next day when he asked where I was, I told him a good, believable story, of course, not the truth!

The next Sunday I drove to Anchorage, and went to my church in order to talk to Ralph Weeks, my pastor, about my experiences, and to tell him I wanted to become a minister. During the church service I thought, after the service when I shake his hand, I cannot talk about such personal things, with so many people listening. I thought, "If he were to ask me for lunch, then I could talk to him about my thinking".

After the service, I shook his hand, and he said, "Oh, by the way, you're invited to lunch at our house today". I was truly surprised, yes, shocked again. Did God, the Holy Spirit speak to me a second time, or were these events only coincidences? At lunch, again I said nothing, because also here, there were too many people at the table to talk so personally. That was my excuse.

The summer went by fast, and I gave no more thought to my experiences. At the end of the summer, I went back to George Fox University in Oregon. At Christmas, again I flew to Anchorage, however this time I spoke with my pastor. He recommended three seminaries, but again I took no action!

Back in Oregon, my roommate asked me one evening what I was going to do after graduation in four months. Both of us were graduating in June. I told him I did not know. I really did not know! I could specialize in wildlife management, which actually was my goal, but I was rather certain I should study theology. I did not want to become a minister, because I did not think I could write well enough, and I was not sure if I was truly a Christian. Some of my ideas and thoughts were not those of some self-styled Christians. I did not want to preach something that was not true, or that I did not believe.

After this talk with my roommate, I went into my room, and thought and thought. I really did not know what I should do with my life. I knew however, I had to make a decision soon. I was absolutely not certain what role Jesus played in history, so I said, though I had these strange, Holy Spirit experiences, Jesus was only a good and helpful man. Period!! Nothing more than that! Jesus was not God! "I will be a biologist, and not a minister!" My decision was final! However, what about my promise? As soon as I said this, I had the worst feeling I have ever had. I felt as if everything had been torn out of me. It was a darkness, which was so black, and empty, I cannot describe it. I had never experienced hell before. This was hell for me, and I hope I never experience it again. Jonah also experienced hell, when he was in the fish's belly.

"But the Lord let a big fish come, that swallowed Jonah. And Jonah was inside the fish 3 days and 3 nights. Then, from inside the fish, Jonah prayed to the Lord his God.... (After Jonah's prayer) the Lord commanded the fish to spit Jonah onto the dry land. A second time God (the Holy Spirit) spoke to Jonah, 'Jonah, go to Nineveh the big city, and preach the Gospel, that I give you'. So Jonah obeyed God, and went to Nineveh."

Jonah prayed with all his strength to God, and asked for forgiveness. He went to Nineveh after God gave him a second chance. He went as a prophet, and messenger of God. Finally, Jonah obeyed his Lord.

After this talk with my roommate, I was very confused. I really did not know the meaning of Jesus. This darkness and emptiness in me was so horrible, that I could not go on living this way without changing my convictions. This experience left such an impression on me, that I realized Jesus was more than just a good and helpful man. Though I did not understand all my feelings and experiences, I had to say, Jesus was also the Christ and God. Then I knelt at my bedside, and prayed as hard as I could that God would forgive me for this unforgivable sin, and that he would take away that dreadful feeling from me. I never prayed so hard in my life. Again, I repeated my promise to become a pastor. God and his Holy Spirit spoke to me a third time. However, this time I obeyed him.

Today I know all Christians have different beliefs, convictions, and various religious understandings. This must be so, since all people have diverse personalities, backgrounds, educations, and different types of intelligences. With all our Christian variances, we can learn from each other and at the same time worship in the same church.

The next day I wrote to three seminaries. At the end of the summer, after several letters back and forth, I received a telephone call from San Francisco Theological Seminary saying I could begin my studies the following Monday. It was already Friday, but Monday morning I flew to San Francisco Theological Seminary in San Anselmo, California, and began studying theology.

Now, dear Christians, this is my personal story. We all have stories to tell, but none are the same, and it is not necessary that we all have such experiences. God, the Holy Spirit, speaks to all of us, but not in the same way, and most of the time, not when we expect it. No matter what happens it is essential that we listen for the Holy Spirit's voice when he speaks to us. Then we need to give him a positive answer. This often requires much strength and courage, but with God's help, and the power of the Holy Spirit, anything is possible. When we ask for God's help, the Holy Spirit will help us!

Today I am very happy that I finally not only heard the Holy Spirit speak, but that, moreover, I responded positively. I said, "Yes, God, I will become a minister". This time I did keep my promise. I really had no other choice except to become a pastor. I know my life would have been empty, if I had not obeyed God and the Holy Spirit.

Prayer:

Dear Lord, please help us to be receptive to your voice. Help us not only to hear you when you speak to us, but also help us to live the life you want us to live. We want to give a positive answer and to follow your guidance. Lead us, so we can do your will and not ours. We pray this in the name of Jesus Christ, our Lord. Amen.

Benediction:

> Lord, our God, creator of the universe, and every living creature within,
> Jesus Christ, our example we are to follow in our daily lives,
> The Holy Spirit, our helper in all times of trouble and sorrow,
> and also in times of joy and happiness,
> Be with every one of us, now and forever. AMEN

What Makes Me a Christian? (Part I)

Seong Nam, Shin Kwang Church, 9.17.2006

Readings: John 6: (59-65) 66-71; Joshua 24:14-18

Text: Matthew 11:28-30 "Come to me, all whose work is hard, whose load is heavy, and I will refresh you. Wear my yoke for it fits perfectly and let me teach you, for I am gentle and humble, and you shall find rest for your souls; for I give you only light burdens."

Today I have chosen a very easy Bible text to understand: "Come to me…" One of the main questions many of us ask sometime in our lives is, "What makes me a Christian?"

"Come to me." Jesus had been visiting the towns scattered around the Sea of Galilee, preaching and healing. Everywhere he had found people in need, not only the crippled, the blind, the epileptics and the lepers, but also the poor, the overworked, the anxious, the frightened and the depressed. As he tried to help the hordes of people, he sensed an even greater need. It was their religious need. When the destitute had faith, their load was lifted. They were given inner strength and thus were able to bear their own burdens easier and help in difficult situations of others. What Jesus found was that the official Jewish religion was actually adding to their dilemmas. For they were told, in order to satisfy God they had to keep rules which were stern and complex. Some felt they could not keep them, so they withdrew from religion altogether. At that point, the religious authorities branded them as "tax-collectors" (a term of abuse in those days) and "sinners", and they spent their lives with the unhappy thought that God had no further use for them. Others tried to keep the Jewish Law, but for the worn-out and the labourers, religious obligations could be like "the straw, that broke the camel's back". Trusting in God seemed for many as an additional burden which was too heavy to carry. Almost the only people Jesus found with a spontaneous, joyful trust in God were the children. That is why he enjoyed having them around him as he talked.

Jesus spoke one day to a crowd on a hillside, and stunned them all by saying: "Come to me, all whose work is hard, whose load is heavy, and I will refresh you." What he was saying was, "I represent a God who doesn't want to add to your load, but rather to lighten it. The conviction I stand for is not to disquiet you, but to lift you up." Christianity is not something we need to carry, but something to carry us. "Come to me, and I will refresh you." That was revolutionary for several reasons.

First, it changed the idea that God was a harsh task-controlling dictator, to a deity who loved them, and was ready to forgive all their sins, and welcome them into his kingdom, where they would find strength, happiness and harmony.

Second, it was radical because Jesus used the word "all" in his invitation. "All" meant more than the reputable, the devout, and meticulous keepers of the Jewish Law. It included the idlers and those who had been alienated by religion. It included the people who had said, "Don't bother me with all that nonsense." "All" included those whom the pious rejected: the tax collectors, prostitutes and Roman soldiers. "Come to me all, whose work is hard", but also, whose work is easy.

Third, this was a ground breaking call, for anyone who has ever said, "Come to me". Yes, even dictators arise who attempt to entice a whole nation. Even some academics, or offbeat leaders, have been so certain about themselves. They seem to be saying, "My philosophy has all the answers. Come to me, and learn from me." However, has anyone ever dared to invite "all", every conceivable type of person in the world, from ancient days until now, September 2006; everyone, past, present and future? "Come to me." No other religious leader has used these words: not Buddha or Mohammed, not Joseph Smith, founder of the Mormon Church, not Mary Baker Eddy, founder of the Christian Science Church, and not even Sun Myung Moon. The most they will say is, "I will show you the God to whom you must come." Jesus said unconditionally, "Come to me".

Those responding in some way to this remarkable offer are called "Christians". The Book of the Acts tells us this was the nickname given to those who followed Jesus. In the early days, the label "Christian" held firmly. If you admitted to being one you risked losing your occupation, your associates, even your existence. Much later, when the Gospel had spread throughout Europe, this Good News also reached entire nations. Almost everyone was baptized, and people spoke of a Christian nation or civilization.

Korea is still in the early stages of Christianity. 250 years ago, there were so-to-speak no Christians in this country. In the time of Jesus, 2000 years ago, the question "Are you a Christian?" meant, "If you're not a Jew, a Moslem, or an agnostic, than you must be a Christian". Today in Korea the question "Are you a Christian?" means, most of the time, "Do you believe in the Jesus as the Christ. Are you a Believer?" This was the original meaning, not "Do you belong to a particular group?"

In the western society, up to now, many Christians have said, "Yes, I am a Christian." They mean, yes, I belong to that particular group. Today however, in some groups in the western world, the question, "Are you a Christian?" has a new meaning, the old meaning. The question has returned to the original meaning, "Are you a believer in Christ, a true or believing Christian? Are you, in fact, one who has come to Him, one who follows Jesus' teachings? "

If you answer "yes", then you should be able to answer the second question. "Why am I a Christian"? I think it is not only important to answer this question, but also is possible to answer it, since there is no entirely correct response.

I will try to express myself in an abridged form and you may do the same. Maybe you are thinking, “Am I truly a Christian?” If this is the case, I hope you will find this sermon and the one next month helpful. Maybe you will hear in a new way what Jesus' words mean: “Come to me”.

The first reason why I am a Christian you might expect. As a pastor, I will offer you all the arguments for believing in Jesus Christ as Lord and Savior. Why am I a Christian? Well, first I studied every reason for and against believing in God. Then, I examined methodically all opposing claims of the great world religions, and I analyzed all the doctrines and church creeds. After I decided Jesus had more of the truth than any other religious scholar had, and when I was content I could learn no more about Jesus, then I became a Christian.

Dear people, all that is absolute nonsense. Truthfully, first, I became a Christian, because I was born to a Christian family, into the Christian tradition.

Does that astonish you? It may sound like a poor reason, but it is the truth. Do you honestly think, if I had been born in a Buddhist community, or a Hindu family, I would have become Christian only by study? Christianity is more than study.

Karl Barth was one of the greatest intellectual theologians of the last century. A colleague of his asked him why he became a Christian, with his perfectly brilliant mind. He replied, “Because my mother told me about Christianity.” Some of you here today would say that family background had a lot to do with why you are Christian. Since Christianity is young in Korea, some of you could not say that. You might say you became a Christian because of personal and spiritual experiences, and because of what you learned from your pastors. Most western Christians became Christian through family connections.

There is nothing wrong with family background and school teachings. We all learned about the universe, other sciences, about mathematics, literature and history. It would have been difficult to learn these things by ourselves. We probably have never questioned the truth of this school information or family inheritance. As far as I myself am concerned, I acknowledge the fact that I was baptized as an infant and taught to pray at an early age. This is certainly one reason why I became a Christian.

Next month I will complete my story of why I am a Christian.

Please always remember, we, in our families, and in our communities, are all continually responsible for teaching Christianity to our children and to those who want to listen. (AMEN)

Prayer: Let us pray.

Again, we gather here today, O Lord. We want to hear your voice. Open our eyes, so we can realize the strength you give to each of us. We want to follow your will, and be the Christians you want us to be. Above all, let us be convinced and know why we are Christians. This is important not only for us personally, but also necessary so we can explain clearly to others your truth and your Good News. In Jesus' name, Amen.

Blessing:

> Lord and God, creator of the universe and all living, and non-living things within,
> Jesus the Christ, the example we are to follow in our daily lives,
> The Holy Spirit, our helper in all that we say and do,
> be with us today, tomorrow and forever.
> In the name of this triune God. AMEN.

What Makes Me a Christian? (Part II)

Seong Nam, Shin Kwang Church, 22.10.2006

Readings: II Corinthians 5:11-17; II Timothy 1:3-9

Text: Matthew 11:28-30 "Come to me and I will give you rest, all of you, who work so hard, beneath a heavy yoke. Wear my yoke, for it fits perfectly. Let me teach you, for I am gentle and humble. You shall find rest for your souls; I give you only light burdens."

"Come to me", said Jesus. What makes me a Christian? We heard last month that my mother was a main reason why I originally became a Christian. She taught me about Jesus, the Bible and praying. Is this "coming to the Lord"?

Of course, this cannot be the whole story. Many people who are baptized and raised in the Christian faith either renounce it later, or just drift away. In addition, many people today come to Jesus, in their maturity, though they had no earlier background in the faith. Obviously, the very first disciples had no such ancestral influence to make them Christians. They came to Jesus on their own, as do some Koreans today, since also these Koreans have had neither Christian parents nor descendants to teach them. Furthermore, most people who have had parental or ancestral influence do not depend on their parents or ancestors as adults, but rather on what they now learn and experience.

My mother taught me the following prayer before going to sleep:

> "Now I lay me down to sleep,
> I pray thee Lord my soul to keep.
> If I should die before I wake.
> I pray thee Lord my soul to take."

The words rhymed, but they frightened me. As a child, I considered the idea that I might die before morning. I thought maybe if I disobeyed my mother or did not do what Jesus wanted I would be punished and perhaps die. I thought I had to follow Jesus or "come to him" in order to live a happy life. When I told my mother the prayer scared me, she taught me "The Lord's Prayer".

As I became older, I realized this was psychologically a poorly written prayer for children. Thus, I changed these stanzas for my children.

> Now I lay me down to sleep.
> I pray thee Lord my soul to keep.
> Guard me Jesus through the night,
> And wake me with the morning light.

As an adult, I continued questioning things about the Bible, God and heaven; things I had learned as a child. Some people told me not to ask so many questions and "believe as a child", but I could not just shut my eyes and believe. Children believe everything their parents tell them as I did. But then children also ask many questions. As I studied theology, my curious intellect told me there was much to learn.

I received a university degree in biology before studying theology. Biology is an exact science; theology is not; therefore, as a scientist, everything had to be proven to me. Thus, I had to deliberate many of my acquired religious teachings.

At an early age I believed I was called into the ministry. However, I had different theological ideas from fundamental Christians, and thought my religious philosophies were wrong. I did not want to preach something from the pulpit which I did not believe. Fortunately, the Holy Spirit began speaking to me very intensely. I finally concluded I could still become a pastor, and preach from the pulpit, even though I had what some might call too liberal or even heretical ideas.

At seminary, I met believers and skeptics. The Holy Spirit continued to speak to me, and my thinking was confirmed that I could become a pastor, and at the same time, preach my own spirituality. I do not mean all my doubts had disappeared, or that I found it easy to bring my religious thoughts into focus with other ideas in my head. This thought process continued during my seminary days, and I have discovered it never ends, thank God.

In addition, now I understand, what people mean when they say, "Just shut your eyes and believe". Similarly, Jesus said, "Believe as a child". If I could not believe, in some ways, as a child, I would not be able to preach on certain topics today, because intellectually I still do not understand them.

However, when asked the question: "What makes you a Christian?" I can say, "I have discovered the Christian understanding of human life, the Christian account of the universe, and the positive results of Christian ethics. They are more intellectually satisfying than other religious or philosophical positions."

That sounds as if this "coming to him" is only from intelligence and education. However, during this learning process, the Holy Spirit has continued to be with me. The scientific world and the spiritual world have worked together to guide me into my Christian understanding. My understanding and response to life today is more complete than it was as a child. I still have questions, but after replying to his "come to me", many things make my life more meaningful and easier to manage, even though there are always problems I must face.

It would be misleading to give the impression that my intellect alone makes me a Christian. Equally as important are my feelings. Why should we be ashamed to admit our emotions are deeply involved in our Christian faith?

In the natural sciences, "objectivity" is significant. In the religious philosophical sciences, "subjectivity" is vital. In Christian decision-making we need both, objectivity and subjectivity, which includes emotions.

When we celebrate Good Friday, for example, I do not find myself thinking about church doctrine, and the atonement, or philosophizing about the sufferings of Christ. I see Jesus on his cross. I hear words like, "Father, forgive them, for they know not what they do." Sometimes I hear a voice saying, "All this I have done for you. What have you done for me?" These mystical words of Jesus' "Come to me" are not just for our intellect. They are a plea to our inner being. These words speak to something deep inside us. Once we really hear his "Come to me", we will have no peace until we humble ourselves and say, "Yes Lord, I come to you". When some of Jesus' followers began disowning him, he asked them, "Will you also go from me?" For those of us who have come to Jesus, he could also ask us this dreadful question.

Recently a small group of politicians (both Christian and Non-Christian) spoke of very personal moments in their lives. They spoke about when they began to understand better their physical being and their nonphysical selves. Unknowingly they were responding to Jesus' invitation, "Come to me". No one spoke of arguments, or doctrines. Everyone had something to say, about a curious and deeply emotional response to the Spirit of Christ, the Holy Spirit.

If we are agitated about political issues, if we become excited about golf or soccer, if we cry at a movie, a play, or a concert, why should we be ashamed to admit Jesus also makes a deeply emotional request of us?

My dear people, emotions are important, but I have neglected something extremely essential. Yes, my background helped to make me a Christian. Yes, my thinking helped lead me to Christianity. Yes, my emotions are strangely aroused by my mystical experiences, and by the Jesus' stories. However, none of this would make me a Christian, unless I had answered his invitation to "come to him".

If a man says to a woman, "I love you. Will you marry me?" she may say to herself, "I know from my background about this marriage business, and I think it's what I want to do. Or: "I've been thinking about him, and I'm convinced he'd make a good husband." Or: "Gee, he really turns me on!" Nevertheless, she will not be his wife until she says, "Yes, I will". If she cannot say those magic words, she is not taking the final step and she will not be married.

A young person at a confirmation ceremony thankfully remembers his family background, and his Christian teachings. He went through a sequence of instructions, over a number of years, in which he used his intellect. Hopefully he also would feel the Holy Spirit calling. If he had, then he could say, "Yes Lord, I come to you." Ultimately, this commitment makes him a Christian, or makes you or me a Christian.

At a confirmation, sometimes there are people sitting in the pews who silently say, "I wish I could also have this opportunity to say, yes Lord, I come to you". This, of course, anyone can do, anywhere, any time, in private or public.

Often, what is lacking in people who want to become Christians is that they have not yet taken that final step. They believe their faith is unstable and unreal, or they are frightened of the future if they confess to Christianity. They know the meaning of their background, their mind, and their emotions, but they have never deliberately used their will, and said that simple, but very difficult, "Yes Lord, I come to you".

You can say today, "Yes Lord, I come", but you must know what you are saying. "I come" involves commitment.

It means, "Yes Lord, lead my life. I will do what you want me to do. I will turn my life over completely and unconditionally to you". I found this last step very difficult. As a young pastor, I did not complete this final step for many years. If we follow God's will, peacefulness is promised us. Today I am happy, because my, "Yes, I come" has led me here to you in Korea. AMEN.

Prayer: Let us pray. First, I will pray and then we will all pray together.

O Lord, speak to all of us today, who are now in your presence. May this be a time, when each of us can say, "Yes Lord, I come to you". Please let us all know, what you mean when you unconditionally say to all of us, "Come to me". Yes Lord, you want all of us, without exception, to "come to you". Give us your blessing, so we can say, "Yes Lord, I come to you". Amen.

Now my dear people, if you, here today, are ready to change your lives and commit yourselves to our Lord or recommit yourselves you may do this. All you need to do is meaningfully say, "Yes Lord, I come to you". If this is your sincere desire, make the commitment by saying, "Yes Lord, I come to you." Now let us all pray together, either silently or aloud, for others and ourselves. "Yes Lord, I come to you". (Prayer Pause)

Thank you Lord for all our decisions today. In Jesus' name, Amen.

“Subject Yourselves to One Another…”

Presbyterian Republic of Korea, Yongjin Presbyterian Church, October 12, 1997

Wedding Sermon

Text: Ephesians 5:21-33

"Wives, be subject to your husbands as to the Lord!" What do you think of that? How can a minister say such a thing? Is it actually true that wives should subject themselves to their husbands? “No, that won’t work”, we say. “Today we are modern. In our time we have ‘Women’s Lib’ and 1975 was ‘the year of the woman’! It is impossible to accept that other nonsense!” Maybe you ask yourself the question, “Why has he chosen precisely this passage as text? It is certainly old fashioned.”

I chose this particular passage because it is often used in wedding ceremonies and often misunderstood. What do we hear when we read Ephesians? Probably only that these women have to do what men want, period. Of course this in not what is meant. Could these words actually say something optimistic to us?

This idea of “Submission”, in today’s world, is so far away from and against our normal thinking that most people must agree this is regression instead of progression in our so-called civilized, social society. Have today’s women not yet reached some kind of equality with men, which is rightfully theirs?

Men and women have always and will always be equal. But we have not recognized this equality, because men and women were put into this world to accomplish different tasks, both of which are equally important. Women have children, because they theoretically can care for them better. They have the female body that is so essential and the motherly instinct.

Some women do not like to hear this, for taking care of a family is sometimes made unrewarding by society. Women are often suppressed, for example they frequently earn less than men for equal work. Occasionally women feel they cannot use their intelligence enough in housework and diaper changing. They believe other professions offer more than homemaking. On the other hand, the fact remains, men cannot give birth to babies! While wives bear children and essentially rear them alone, it is necessary for husbands to earn money to provide for the family.

We are very materialistic people. Since the husband brings the money home, he is worth more, or at least so we often think. However, it is definitely as important to have a nice home and well-kept family. Statistics show that if women did their housework properly and if they were paid the same amount per hour as men, they would or should earn the equal salary. Both have equally important responsibilities, but not the same ones.

“Wives ‘be subject to’ or ‘be submissive to’ or ‘regard (respect) your husbands…” is found written in the different biblical translations. A woman can make a man happy and help him, but it should not become an obligation. She ought to stand by her husband, because of her love for him and also to please herself. When wives wish to serve their husbands, that is virtuous, however if it is done under pressure and they feel forced to be good to their husbands, then it is done in vain. But how can a woman, according to Paul, the apostle, be satisfied when she has to submit herself to her husband? That, dear people, depends on the husband!

In our scripture Paul writes not only about wives, but also about husbands. “Husbands, love your wives in the same way that Christ loved the Church and gave his life for it.” This means, the man should care for his wife with a pure, lasting, unconditional love that only comes from God, otherwise it is all useless. When husbands love their wives as Jesus loved his fellowman, wives can feel such love and they will gladly be here when their husbands need and want them, but is this the only valid relationship between a man and a woman? No, also in reverse, when women love their men to the same depth, then men, in the similar fashion perceive a woman’s love. Paul writes, “Wives, regard (respect) your husbands!” Also he writes, “Husbands, love your wives!” What does that in fact mean, that wives should not love their husbands and husbands should not respect their wives? No, of course not, both should love, respect and mutually work in partnership with each other. Paul simply emphasizes that the husband love his wife and the wife respect her husband and be at his side, not that one excludes the other.

When a man and a woman live in a mutual relationship of love, and each person submits himself to the other for the partner’s wellbeing, then at the same time their lives resemble a circle that continually becomes larger and more complete in love and understanding for each other.

But how is it with people who say, “I am not going to do this or that for my spouse, because he didn’t do it for me.” Or one thinks of the other, “I am not going to help her because she wouldn’t help me”. Or even, “I suspect my spouse may have betrayed me, therefore I will betray him too“. My friends, how does love decrease? How does hate increase?

It is nice for example, when we see Korean women, how they serve their husbands. But it is not so nice when they serve them only because of tradition. That is not what Paul means. Paul emphasizes that husbands ought not to rule over and demand submissiveness from their wives, instead a relationship should be developed whereby there should be a mutual give and take. They should not only demand rights from each other but also give rights and together take on the many different responsibilities. Only when a couple can jointly co-operate with each other, only when they live in God’s love, will they be able in peace and joy to build a Christian home.

That sounds very easy. All we have to do is follow the rules and everything will always remain fine. But in reality it is not that simple. There will always be conflicts and disagreements, and times when one will want to control the other, maybe sometimes unconsciously. The time may even come when the couple thinks it is useless to continue a life together. When it comes to this point then it is necessary for us all to look at the vows we took earlier as we were married. "...in plenty and in want, in joy and in sorrow, in sickness and in health, through all the years we are given." But most important, before this moment is reached, talk with each other. Discuss your problems openly and always be 100% honest with your spouse, if you both really want to stay together! I am sure your partner will try to understand and help in any way possible. In most cases complications can be found in each partner, not merely in one or the other.

Until now we have only examined verse 22, "Wives, be submissive/subject to your husbands" and verse 25, "Husbands, love your wives". In our times of rapid change we find, among other things, changing family roles. For example we find women working outside the household and men, who stay at home taking care of their children. Maybe the wife earns more or her profession is more meaningful to her than her husband's occupation is to him. Why couldn't we say in this case, "Husbands, be submissive to your wives" and "wives, love your husbands", for in verse 21 we read, "Submit yourselves to one another, because of your reverence for Christ". And that is what is important. Only through the love of Christ can we love and be true to each other. That is, only when we love our fellowman, our spouses, as Jesus, in his time, loved those people, are we able to live a happy, meaningful and rewarding life with our partner. For this reason we have a Christian wedding.

Yes, we see that both individuals should love and submit themselves to each other. When both, in God's love, live for one another, they will experience a continuously growing love. That is, when they love and serve God in their fellowman and their spouse, when they mutually co-operate with one another, then they will develop a good, solid and rewarding relationship in their future together. They will be happy and become real companions.

If you and I know that we are here for each other, then to be submissive means "accepting a person as he is". When we understand "submission" as something positive, then being subject to one another is full of our own personality and full of the trust we have in and for our spouse. It is not negative. It is something which becomes very positive, that no one can destroy.

____(Bride's name)____will you submit yourself to ____(Groom's name)____.

____(Groom's name)__are you so close to God, do you love____(Bride's name)____so much that she will want to be submissive to you?

____(Groom's name)___will you submit yourself to_____(Bride's name)_____.

____(Bride's name)__are you so close to God, do you love____(Groom's name)____so much that she will want to be submissive to you?

These questions are not merely directed to a newly wedded couple, but rather are questions addressed to every couple, young and old.

Are you willing to submit yourselves to one another in love, as Jesus submitted himself, on the cross, out of his love for us? Or in today's language, are you willing to stand by your mate through all parts of life, both in good and bad times? That is the most important, — to live for your helpmate. In Jesus' name, Amen.

How Christians Disagree

Seong Nam, Shin Kwang Church, 10.30.2008

Text: Colossians 3: 12-17 (Life Application Bible: The Living Bible)

"Most of all, let love guide your life, for then the whole church will stay together in perfect harmony. Let the peace of heart which comes from Christ be always present in your hearts and lives, for this is your responsibility and privilege as members of the body. (Christian Church). Always be thankful." (Colossians 3:14-15)

Readings: Proverbs 15: 1-26; Mark 9: 33-37

What happens when Christians disagree? Love, unity, peace, and thankfulness — these are the main points the Christian community should observe when disagreement occurs. Jesus said in John 13: 34-35, "...I am giving a new commandment to you now: love each other just as much as I love you. Your strong love for each other will prove to the world that you are my disciples".

Jesus' apostles continued reminding the new churches that they were united in love, peace and appreciation. John told the new Christians that they had always heard, from the beginning, the message: Love one another. Paul wrote to them that they should make every effort to secure the promise of harmony, which the Spirit gives them. Peter voiced that they should be in one belief and understanding, and be full of companionable love, compassion and humility. James declared to his people that God's wisdom was unadulterated, peaceable, kind and rational. There is no question that the early Christian Church could live in harmony, inspired by love, peace and thankfulness. We also can live in harmony even with the church's power struggles, dogmas and disagreements, if we let the Spirit work in us.

But let us look at our church history. There were violent disagreements which tore the Church apart. There were theological fights, ecclesiastical arguments and vicious conflicts between Christians. Look at the reformation in Europe; the violent fighting between Catholics and Protestants. Think of the famous Swiss reformer, Huldrych Zwingli. He was brutally murdered in the name of the Christian Church when he was torn apart by four horses, tearing his arms and legs off his body. Religious wars such as the Crusades caused uncountable deaths. Middle Age witch-hunts in the name of Christianity also caused innocent deaths and unbelievable misery and pain to families and communities. Read the newspapers today and watch television, see all the tragedies of terrorism in the name of religion. These are stories of bitterness, division, strife and discontent rather than of love, unity, peace, and thankfulness.

What can we say? We can say nothing to excuse these actions. This is the unfaithfulness of the dream of Jesus and his followers. However, this story of the early Church is not a total denial of the positive actions of the Church in that era. It is not a complete failure to obey the Gospel. The Christian Church was also the founder of institutions of love and care, organizations, such as schools, hospitals, orphanages and places of refuge. This church too produced great works of art, which depicted acts of affection, worship and care for the disadvantaged. This same church brought forth many saints, who released the adoration and harmony of Christ. The Reformation disorder was not completely damaging. Some of the best Christian minds and philosophers were born. It produced social communities of Christian love and concern. Unfortunately, today in the media we often hear of scandal and division in the Church. Rarely do we hear a story of healing or a uniting movement in the Church.

We must acknowledge that Christians disagree and have always disagreed. There are also disagreements here in Shin Kwang and in other Christian churches in Korea and elsewhere. But this is normal and also good. We have to eliminate the myth that we have no disagreements and that we should always totally agree with each other. We have to eliminate the myth that in New Testament times all was harmony and contentment. Many of Jesus' followers, who heard his words and saw his actions of love, quarreled amongst themselves. Even Jesus' twelve Apostles who were filled with the Spirit, sometimes had quite violent disagreements.

Early Christians often failed to live according to their own standards. We also have failed to live according to Jesus' teachings. However, living according to Jesus' teachings does not mean we must always agree. Differences are not always bad. Jesus certainly did not expect his followers always to be in total agreement. That would not only be uninteresting, but also unproductive. Christian disagreement can be very creative and fruitful. A Christian life with disagreement makes Christians more alive, more genuine and more distinctly individual. Thus, Christians will have different opinions and different visions. This is good and it is surely possible for Christians to differ without being unpleasant.

Disagreement is a portion of human freedom. Disagreement is part of the price we pay for our rights and choices. Our brothers and sisters in North Korea are not allowed to disagree. If they disagree with the government they are put in jail; they are deprived of their dignities and the necessities of life or they may be tortured and often killed. There will obviously be more disagreement and conflict of opinion in a true democracy than in communism.

In an active church, we should never have to hide our differences. In an active church, no one should be afraid to say, "I disagree". The same truth holds for families and all social societies. Wearing masks of total agreement will not avoid disputes, and squabbles. Arguments and fights are avoided by the freedom to be different, and the willingness to disagree in the spirit of love, compassion and understanding. Paul believes that Christ's peace should rule in the heart.

Colossians 3: 14-15 not only says we need to be controlled by love and peace but also it is essential for us to be thankful. A thankful person is one who is grateful to God for everything including being grateful for disagreement. Disagreements can be seen in relationship to the entire situation. Disagreements are solved when the betterment of the society and its people are considered. Disagreements are not solved when we think of just ourselves. Thankful people also see disagreements with a sense of some humor. This prevents the insignificant from becoming swollen into a large conflict. An English proverb states: "Don't make a mountain out of a molehill". Similarly, the power of Jesus' love and peace keeps disagreement from sliding into hostility, bitterness and rival groups. We hear enough about feuds and rival groups in all sections of the Christian church. Often not seen are the beautiful times known to all who have worked in active churches. These active churches live according to our text: "Always be thankful." They are thankful for opposing views even if they are firmly and passionately stated. In such churches the necessary unity and peace of a church is preserved with a spirit of common respect and love for each other. This is the wonder of beauty, charm and grace. This is the asset of a united Christian family.

Why do we have more than 100 different Presbyterian Churches here in Korea? The Presbyterian Church has split into so many pieces because there are differences and frequent church disagreements, many of which are surely minor. Our difficulty comes when we try to distinguish between what is vital and what is supplementary. When these religious disagreements are crucial to our Christian belief, when these differences interact with our Christian faith, we are often more aroused than we are when other issues of difference occur, such as car color, or shoe style. Thus, there will be times of Christian disagreement, which are serious and cannot be hidden by tolerant indifference. This was true when Paul led the fight against all who wanted to make Gentile converts keep the Jewish Law. The Christian religion was in danger. Also the church was split by what was called the "Arian heresy". As a result of this conflict, the Nicene Creed was written, which states that Christ is truly human and truly divine. If the Arians had won this conflict, we would be worshiping neither a truly human, nor a truly divine, Christ.

Another major difference occurred during the Reformation period. However, it was not a matter of whether or not we should pray in Latin or what robes the pastor should wear or from where he should speak, for example, from the pulpit or from the baptismal fount. The fundamental difference was, "Do we need a mediator other than Christ?" The Protestants said "no"; the Catholics said "yes", we need a priest.

In our society it takes much vision to differentiate where the fundamentals of our Christianity are being challenged. There will always be times when Christians must risk the consequences of disagreement. But the question is, "How do Christians disagree?" Do we disagree with love and understanding? Do we want the best for our family, community, society and the world? Or do we say, "I want what I want, when I want it!"

Surely those who threaten to divide a congregation or split a denomination should think and pray seriously and have a little humor before they break a spiritual union and before they split a church. Humor means, "Is this disagreement really necessary; is it so minor that it is a little ridiculous to argue over". Do we truly win when we make "a mountain out of molehill", when we destroy a Christian union? What is best for the community, the family, the sports club, the political group, or the church? Am I right when I want a change or am I only thinking of myself? Remember, sometimes change is not necessary; we can always learn from our differences.

Differences and changes can mean renewed vitality, make helpful advancements and make new visions, if we learn in thankfulness and humility to keep our minds and personalities open to the acceptance of Jesus' teachings of peace and love. I truly believe we should all be able to worship in the same church with many minor differences. We are all Christians here in Shin Kwang Church. We all have faith in the Triune God and we all believe for what God stands. This is important; not the many minor differences. What the pastor wears, a suit or clerical robe, or where he stands, at the baptismal fount or in the pulpit, is minor. What he says is major. So, let us smile and have a little humor with our minor differences!

When living in this world with all cultures the most important thing is to love one another. The apostle Paul said, "I may speak in tongues of men, or of angels, but if I am without love, I am a sounding gong, or a clanging cymbal" (1. Corinthians 13:1). Today, in Christian differences, we often hear only the sounding gong and the clanging cymbal. Nevertheless, thank God, we can also hear the prayers of those who live according to these commanding words, "Most of all, let love guide your life, for then the whole church will stay together in perfect harmony. Let the peace of heart which comes from Christ be always present in your hearts and lives, for this is your responsibility and privilege as members of the body. (Christian Church). Always be thankful."

Prayer:

O God, we are thankful for Christian harmony and friendship between us. Let us have courage and be open and honest with each other. Let us always listen and make decisions in Christian love for the good of our fellow mankind. We want to seek the agreement which Christianity has given our Church. Be with us all, when we face differences, and let us find true peace through our Lord. In his name, Amen.

About Heaven

Seong Nam, Shin Kwang Church, 16.11.2008; Dubai, United Arab Emirates, Kwanglim Church, 30.11.2008

Text: I. John 3:2-3:

"My dear people, we are already the children of God, but what we are to be in the future has not yet been revealed; all we know is that when it is revealed, we shall be like him, because we shall see him as he really is. Surely everyone who entertains this hope must purify himself, must try to be as pure as Christ." (Jerusalem Bible)

"Are you certain you would go to heaven, if you died today?"

I think it would be difficult for me to ask a stranger this question. I am not even certain God would want me to make such an inquiry. Jesus did not ask this question nor did his disciples. Someone might answer, "I'm uncertain about my going to heaven, but I surely hope so". Another might respond, "That's a personal question and it's none of your business." In either case, I would appreciate and accept his reply.

However, I do think this is a vital question and I have talked with many people about heaven. These talks have been very rewarding for all of us. Nevertheless, often on pastoral visits our discussions have only been about trivial matters. Many times, I think this has been a mistake. Often people want to discuss death, dying and heaven, but they are afraid to ask such questions. Concerns about eternal life have much to do with our Christian lives today as it did in the past. Here in Shin Kwang Church, we regularly say the Apostles Creed, "I believe in the resurrection of the body and the life everlasting."

Is this affirmation just a way of saying, "This has always been the Church's belief so I will agree with it even if it's not truly part of my belief"? On the other hand, do I say, "Well, maybe it's true and maybe it's not, but I hope it is?" Perhaps I say, "Heaven isn't relevant to me but many people, whom I admire including Jesus himself, past saints and scholars, and some valued friends, have found eternal life to be absolutely real. Thus, I hope an unending life will also become real to me." Here are some of my questions and thoughts: "What would be the purpose of my insignificant life, if it ended with my earthly death? What can convince me of a never-ending life? How can I go from the vague 'hope' to the definite 'know'? I do know there is some kind of heaven to which I am headed but actually what?"

Just because we live in an age of technology and space-exploration does not mean the inquiry into perpetual life no longer exists. Today there is an astonishing recurrence of accounts, debates and examinations on the topic of death and its significance for us. We are all interested in life and death. If we knew there would be an atomic war tomorrow, all the churches would be filled with only one question: "What do we do now?"

According to Biblical understandings and Church teachings, we know little about eternal life. Some say, "The Bible is a book about heaven and it gives detailed information about the afterlife. Some say if we want knowledge about the world, scientists and historians give us this information and for understanding about the next life, the Bible gives us this comprehensive data. Well if you believe this, you will be disappointed. Ninety per cent of the Bible is about life here and now, about its chaos and adventures, about its beauty and violence, about its laws, morals and economics, and about its loves and hates. There are very few references, even vague references, to eternal life in the Old Testament and we know in Jesus' time, the Sadducees, who were strictly orthodox, rejected eternal life completely. (Luke 20:27)

In the New Testament however, Jesus took for granted that we were headed for a new life beyond the cemetery. He told his disciples, "There are many dwelling-places in my father's house; if it were not so, I would have told you; for I am going there on purpose to prepare a place for you." (John 14:2). He discouraged any inquisitiveness about the next life.

When the Sadducees told Jesus that story about the woman who had had seven husbands and asked him whose wife she would be "at the resurrection", he considered this question irrelevant, only saying we could not transfer earthly conditions to heavenly conditions. (Luke 20:27-39) Since we know virtually nothing about heaven and angels, it is impossible for anyone to value the life beyond.

After Jesus' resurrection, his apostles were zealously committed to the fact that heaven was ahead of them. They believed Paul's words, "neither death, nor life, nor angels, nor principalities, nor powers, nor things present, nor things to come, nor height, nor depth, nor any other creature, shall be able to separate us from the love of God, which is in Christ Jesus our Lord" (Romans 8: 38-39). Nevertheless, none of the apostles had any precise evidence about paradise and spiritual messengers. Paul was only able to say we would have a "spiritual body".

This sounds like a contradiction, when we understand the Bible as telling us we will have a physical resurrection. However, is a physical body in heaven the same as a physical body on earth? Is a physical body in heaven also a spiritual body? In heaven, are the physical and spiritual bodies integrated? Again, we do not understand heavenly things and we cannot transfer heavenly conditions to earthly conditions.

In the Book of Revelation, we read about the popular idea of crowns, streets of gold, melodious harps, magnificent choirs and gleaming jewels. Its author is writing in the inspiring imagery of Jewish apocalypse, the Judgement Day and the end of the world. He would be surprised to learn that his visions were being understood literally.

For me the most satisfying Bible statement about heaven is what is written in our text. "We are already the children of God". "We," addresses a Christian congregation, a group of people as varied as we are, here in our church, with various degrees of righteousness and irreverence, truthfulness and unfaithfulness, and justice and unfairness, but unified in a promise to Jesus Christ. "We are the children of God," indicates that God does not let his children stray away from him or let them go. God will keep us by him despite our immoral activities. We will always be near God even when our body dies. Jesus said our Lord was God of the living, not of the dead, for to him all of us are alive, even in death we are still alive. We know we are God's children and nothing can pull us away from Him.

Then our text says, "What we are to be in the future has not yet been revealed." This is a hurtful and blunt statement, which has led some to scepticism or disbelief. If we really understood this text, the future would be certain for us. We would know definitely that at this time the future remains hidden from us. We just do not know about heaven and the future.

In Switzerland, when baptising a child, I take him in my arms and sometimes say, "This is the love our heavenly Father has given us; we are called 'children of God'". I know this baby is a child of God. What I do not know and what the parents do not know is what will become of this child. "What we are to be in the future has not yet been revealed." This also means, what heaven is like "has not yet been revealed" to us. Christian faith makes no claim to predict what kind of beings we will be in eternity, what we will look like, what abilities we will have or how we will spend our time. Eternity "has not yet been revealed"!

We know nothing about heaven; essentially nothing! However, when we die, heaven will be revealed. Meanwhile here on earth, we do however know one thing about heaven. Verse 3 says, "We shall be like him". There is no scepticism, no doubt and no hesitancy in our text. We know we will be like him. In the original Greek translation and every other biblical translation of which I am aware, with all their differences, they each agree on one thing, "We will be like him". This is what Christians know about heaven. We will be like Jesus Christ! There is no other place in the Bible which allows us to say that we know something about heaven, except for this conviction: We will be in the presence of God. In His presence we will equal his personality, as it is revealed in Jesus Christ, his Son.

This is a breath-taking thought, to be like Jesus! Is it actually possible to be like Jesus? Yes it is, but not in this world. What does this truly mean for us? Could it mean our new bodies will be like the resurrection body of Jesus?

Truthfully, heaven is a growing place for us. In heaven, we can grow into God's image, into the likeness of Jesus Christ. However, all luxurious pictures of a heaven, such as gold-plated sports cars, the life of the rich with their luxurious yachts and summer mansions, are excluded. Heaven is becoming like Jesus Christ, becoming like his abundant love for every creature, becoming like his joy for human relationship, becoming like his sense of magnificence and mystery, becoming like his desire for fairness, and becoming like his vision of peace. This depicts Jesus' pureness. Jesus said, "Blessed are the pure in heart, for they shall see God" (Mathew 5:8). On earth, we can begin to become "pure in heart", and in heaven we can continue our journey on becoming "pure in heart".

What is heaven? Heaven is about becoming like Jesus, about being as pure as Jesus!

I cannot describe the sociology or draw the landscape of heaven. Nevertheless, I can tell you we know Christ is there and that miraculously, "we will be like him"! This does not mean we will all be duplicate personalities living in a paradise of monotony. Jesus said, "In my father's house are many rooms". Nevertheless, more important, Jesus said, "Father, I want those you have given me to be with me where I am" (John 17:24).

He is there with all of his magnificence and with all he will mean to you and me. That is all I need to know! With this enlightenment, I can live a full and satisfying life on earth and hope to serve the people around me as Jesus did, thus beginning to become as pure as Christ.

Is it actually essential for us to become "pure in heart", pure in Spirit, as is Christ? Why should we be concerned about our purity, if we know we will be in God's company? Does the knowledge we have about heaven have any consequence on our everyday lives? Is this awareness a type of life protection policy to be kept safe and then exchanged for eternal life when we leave this earth? Our text responds: "Surely everyone who entertains this hope must purify himself, must try to be as pure as Christ". In other words, as Christians we have the knowledge and conviction about heaven and living a life as pure as Jesus. Now we must act.

This should be a moral power directing our lives now on earth and in this church. In the end, when we have this knowledge about heaven and are convinced of a life as pure as is Jesus, we know our entire life now is going in this direction, in the heavenly direction. This knowledge and certainty about heaven and a life pure in soul and spirit is the practical assistance we as Christians have to ultimately satisfy and support our daily lives. We know that we are going somewhere, that we are headed with others toward the purity of life and soul, which we see in Christ. Christians want to go in this direction. Christians want to live their lives for others. Christians want to value love, goodness and compassion. This is living a life "pure in heart". This is living in the purity of Christ.

Although our text tells us we will be like Jesus, it does not tell us if we will reach the same purity in soul as Jesus.

"My dear people, we are already the children of God, but what we are to be in the future has not yet been revealed; all we know is that when it is revealed, we shall be like him, because we shall see him as he really is. Surely everyone who entertains this hope must purify himself, must try to be as pure as Christ."

Prayer:

Dear Lord, we want to live a life pure in soul. Help us today, here on earth and here in Shin Kwang Church, to begin to live this life as "pure as Christ". We want to continue this journey in heaven and strive toward the goal of being pure in spirit, as is Christ. We know being like Christ is living in joy and peace. In Jesus' name, Amen.

To Die Is To Live

Funeral Sermon

Text: John 11, 17- 44

When I read in the newspapers or hear about friends and relatives who have died, and are the same age or younger than I, I begin to ask myself how much longer I have here on earth. What more does the future hold for me? Do I have good years or suffering ones? As a pastor, I have talked with people who are afraid to die, because they do not know about eternity. Some believe when their earthly lives end they have nothing more to expect, thus for them there is no future truth of any kind.

Our scripture describes the entrance of Jesus into Bethany, where Lazarus died four days earlier. According to the Hebrew tradition, the spirit hovers close to the body three days after the person's death in hopes that the body and soul would reunite and again become a living person. However after three days, when the body begins to decay, the spirit leaves. In the case of Lazarus, the fourth day was important, because the Hebrews believed it was impossible for the body and soul to reunite once the body begins to decompose. Since Jesus raised Lazarus physically on the fourth day, the miracle was even greater.

Today however we want to concern ourselves with a spiritual resurrection more so than with a bodily rebirth. Jesus also meant a spiritual reawakening. Mary and Martha wanted and expected a bodily revival. They were angry with Jesus since he was only about two miles away in Jerusalem and still did not come to the deathbed of Lazarus until the fourth day. Their thinking was that now a bodily rebirth would not be possible. Jesus said to Martha, "Your brother will be resurrected". She believed Jesus and said, "I know he will be resurrected on the last day, on Judgment day." This belief was very common among the pious Pharisees and other Israelites. Jesus did not criticize or expel the Pharisees for their belief, but he wanted Martha and all others to know from where their current and spiritual life came. At this time, Jesus was not concerned with a life on Judgment Day. He said, "I am the resurrection and the life. If anyone believes in me, even though he (physically) dies he will (spiritually) live, and whoever lives and believes in me will never die." That is, whoever has unconditional trust in Jesus will have eternal life. Not only is a last day resurrection important. A spiritual resurrection today is equally significant and we can all know and experience this unknown, mystical, spiritual renewal today.

Martha was of course very sad she had lost her brother. Our wonderment grows when we observe how the discussion continued. Martha was peaceful and self-controlled. It is not easy to explain her solid spiritual strength, trust, and faith. We can understand that she had the deep hope Jesus would come within three days for a bodily resurrection. It was of particular disappointment for Martha since Jesus, Lazarus, Mary and she had developed a very close relationship over the years. Logically, they believed Jesus would come. When he did not arrive until the fourth day, we can understand the disapproval in Martha's voice. "If you had been here my brother would not have died, but I know that even now, whatever you ask of God, he will grant you". She probably did not know the exact meaning of her statement, but she knew God could do anything he wished.

Even though earthly life can be enjoyable and worthwhile, we cannot find the ultimate in our being until our physical bodies leave this world. We do not understand everything that comes from God, but we do know if we ask him for faith, and if we trust him, we will receive power to live according to his will and courage to witness for him. We will then find fulfillment and peace.

Death is always difficult for us to understand. We do not know when or why a person must leave his earthly body. Both life and death come to us for an unknown reason and from an unidentified source. Through biology, chemistry and physics we might be able to explain the source of our existence but the purpose for our reality remains unclear for many. I call this unknown force "God". All we know is with every birth there is a death. However, dear people, with physical death comes new life, a spiritual life that is overwhelming and unimaginable. Even though this new life is unknown to us, we know from our text and other Bible verses, all believers have consecrated eternal lives, which can begin here on earth. Happiness, peace and harmony are Christian rewards, when we have love and compassion for all humankind, including strangers, refugees and others we do not know, or may not understand or appreciate.

This new and consecrated eternal life is in us when joy and love radiate from us. Love glows and flows from our faces. We now have a life showing kindness and understanding for all around us. We can feel the energy surging from those, having new life.

When I was about eleven years old and shortly before my grandmother died, she said with great wisdom, "I am ready to die". She continued, "You know, once I think about everything, I will be happy to die." Can you imagine what I thought, as an 11-yearold child? How can someone want to die? What could I say? She maintained that there was a much better reality when one only has a soul. It is a completely different life. It is not describable, understandable and it is not even accurately thinkable. Only after death can we experience the second part of eternal life.

Do we have the faith to accept death, when it comes our way? Even though for some it is not easy to believe these biblical words, God will help our faith when we ask for his guidance and care.

I have memories of a 17-year-old boy I met, when I was a chaplain at Pacific Medical Center in San Francisco in 1971. He was crippled and was a flower child, or hippy, of those days. I visited him often. During one of our conversations he said, "If I were dead I would be freed from my physical body and could walk or move about with ease". He meant at that time, he could not walk or easily maneuver some of his body parts.

I believe his understanding and faith was, in some way, strong enough for him to know there was something more beyond this life. Maybe he had a little vision of what comes as an immortal being.

I am convinced that my grandmother and this young man, if he is no longer alive, are now living eternal, spiritual lives. I am also certain that when you and I leave our earthly bodies we will have spiritual forms. Jesus said, "I am the resurrection and the (eternal) life. He who believes in me, even though he dies he will live, and whoever lives and believes in me will never die".

Dear worshipers, "to die is to live". AMEN!

Benediction:

May the Lord bless you and keep you,
May the Lord let his face shine upon you,
and be gracious unto you,
May the Lord lift up his countenance upon you,
and give you peace until we meet again.
In the name of Jesus Christ, our Lord. Amen.

More Life is Joy

Seong Nam, Shin Kwang Church, 23.10.2011

Funeral Sermon

Readings: Hebrews 12: 2; John 15: 1–11

Text: Psalm 30, 5: "His anger lasts a moment; his favor lasts a life! Weeping may go on all night (in this life), but in the morning there is joy (with God - on earth and in heaven)."

Here is a dialogue between two deceased people,

> "Now you have experienced death," said the elderly gentleman. "Is it good?"
> "It is good!" said the other. "It's better than life."
> "No," said the elderly gentleman, "It's more life!"

More life! The Christian news about life beyond the cemetery centers on being close to God, not just on having more and more of simple life.

§In recent years, there has been interest in psychic evidence about life continuing after death. People, who have been clinically dead for a few minutes, say they have experienced this life beyond. However, even if it could be proven that life continues after death, the Christian would not rejoice, since he has known this for the past two thousand years. The New Testament shows no interest in a simple infinite existence. It is interested in an eternal life, according to Jesus. It is interested in this "more life".

When we define heaven as "more life" it is earthly life we are talking about, our inner life, this life that Christ brings, this life that is nurtured and sustained by God, this life we see supremely in Christ. Jesus was life and Jesus' life was and is in man. The Good News tells us, we have this life now, as we live in God's grace. It tells us death is the entrance to "more life". We read, "He, who believes in the Son, has eternal life." It is more of our earthly life that lies beyond this life, more of God's love, more of these wonderful times of complete spiritual union with God, more of the contentment we know in human warmth, more of the fulfillments that come to us in our search for morality, truth, and splendor.

Imagine if someone came and gave you a quantity of limitless life after passing into the next world. This endless eternity would be like the life you knew on earth, when you were the furthest from God. Nothing would matter except your comfort and joy. Your days would have no real meaning, no direction, no challenge, and no inner life, only your trouble-free life. You maybe would say, "This is hell you are giving me."

But suppose he gave you a definite amount of endless existence of that life you knew when God was near, when you really cared about others, when your suffering changed into joy, and despair into hope. Would you not want to say, "Yes, that would be good — more of that life."

The psalmist said, "... his favor lasts for life!" He did not just mean that we exist; that our hearts beat by God's grace. He meant our unsurpassed existence lies in this jubilant belief and confidence we have in God. The whole verse reads like this in the Psalms, "His anger lasts for a moment, his favor lasts for life." The unrest, which we so often experience, comes from our non-dependence on God. Unless we know his love and unless we acknowledge his presence, we can only know his displeasure and the problems in our lives. However, when we turn to God, we recognize our life is grounded and elevated in Christ and that we can in no way compare it to life's end.

Among other things, life is prayer, worship, and fellowship. After death we are promised more of this radiant life beyond. However, what is "more life"? Sometimes we picture heaven as a state of constant boredom and tedious worship, which never ends. If there is "more life" in heaven, does the New Testament give us a clue as to what it encompasses?

Little is said about heaven in the New Testament and the Old Testament says essentially nothing. That is certainly because as human beings, we are not capable of comprehending that new dimension. Jesus only said we would be like the angels and we know not what angels are like.

I thought there must be some hint as to what this afterlife might be like. The elderly gentleman seemed to know when he said, "The hereafter is 'more life'". In addition, many texts including the gospels, the epistles, and the Book of Revelation proclaim the same message that "more life" is "joy". For Jesus, it was obvious that the content of eternal life was "joy".

We discover from the New Testament that the first Christians supported and were alive in this same "joy". The early Christian Church from its beginning was probably separated from the surrounding culture, perhaps more by joy, than anything else. We are told in the Book of Acts, that when the disciples had been arrested, delivered to the Council, and warned to stop speaking about Jesus, "They departed from the presence of the Council, rejoicing, that they were counted worthy to suffer shame for his name. And daily in the temple, and in every house, they ceased not to teach, and to preach Jesus."

Are we like the disciples, or are we accustomed to a grim, puritanical picture of Christianity, which we think takes the joy out of our lives? If so, it's a shock to us when we realize that Christianity puts joy into our lives.

It was a sad, terrified world into which the Good News came, and nowhere was the disciples' joy more impressive and inconceivable to the pagans, than when they, the disciples, faced death.

When Paul realized he would probably be led from prison to execution, he confessed that he had two desires. On the one hand, he longed to go on living in order to complete his lifework. On the other hand, he wanted to depart from earth, and be with Christ — which he said was far better. It is in his prison letters, with death near, that he speaks most of joy. His whole Christian life was sustained by the conviction that though "weeping may endure for a night, joy comes in the morning."

So it was with Peter, with John and all who have left us their witness to the faith. None of them offered much information about heaven, but they were all certain that it was what Peter called "joy unspeakable", joy indescribable.

I believe sincerely the seal of the Christian Church is the belief in this continuous, inconceivable joy beyond death. This "joy" is "more life".

But I ask you, is this just the religious version of our love for a story with a happy end? It could be, if we didn't take seriously the weeping at a funeral. None of us is spared the agony of the darkness, when we have to "walk through the valley of the shadow of death". We are not asked to behave as though death were a mere incident to be quickly forgotten. Rather, the Bible encourages us to see death as an enemy, before whose power we bow in tears. Then, when we have been to our Calvary, we are ready to experience our Resurrection. The Lord comes to us, and we know our end is "joy".

Jesus knew the night of weeping, not just because he would die, but he wept for those who were to kill him. He wept for all of us for our foolishness, for our shortcomings, for our lack of trust in God. He wept for those who might miss the "joy" at the end of their life. How Jesus could endure all this agony is a mystery. But Jesus trusted, and had faith in his God, even though on that Thursday night he was betrayed; even though on that Friday death and darkness covered Golgotha, and the women wept. Then, on that Sunday morning early, there was a great shouting of joy. No other joy has ever been as powerful, and wonderful as this joy.

Yes, before morning comes to us, before we experience this morning joy in our lives, all of us have to experience the blackness of night. Finally, at death, we shall be in the perfect joy of God's presence, where "There shall be no more death, neither sorrow, nor crying, neither shall there be any more pain; for the former things are passed away."

Are we ready to accept this promise of supreme joy, which lies beyond death? Or do we still cling to the notion that duty and seriousness belong to the presence of God, and joy is merely secondary?

Sometimes we think Christianity and joy do not go together. The question is, do we so trust in the One who wishes more life for us? Are we so constantly open to the grace of our Lord Jesus Christ, so open to the power of his Spirit, that our death will be the entrance to this heaven of continuous, incomparable joy?

It is not possible for me to believe we shall experience this fullness of joy only here on earth. Just as we have learned concerning the highest joys that human life can offer, certainly we will learn about the unending joys in God's heavenly presence. For "the eye has not seen, nor the ear heard....the things which God has prepared for them, who love him." We love God when we love our fellowmen, when we follow Jesus' teachings. To follow the life of which the Bible speaks, we need to be continually nourished by our Lord. Then, at our end, which is our beginning, we will experience this unending, this most powerful, and magnificent joy of the heavenly Kingdom. AMEN.

Prayer:

Dear Lord, be with us and give us the wisdom and spiritual guidance we need to experience the joy of "more life" here on earth and in the life to come. Help us to follow your teachings of love. Nourish us so we can live for our mankind. After we have found "more life" on earth, we want also to find "more life" in heaven. Oh Lord, be with us eternally. In Jesus' name, Amen.

Benediction:

God, be gracious unto us and bless us.
God, may your face shine upon us,
God, may your ways be known to us on earth and in heaven.
God, may your saving power be known among all nations. AMEN. (Psalm 67:1-2)

Life After Life: Biblical Confirmation Through the Back Door

(The Bible is the front door.)

Seong Nam, Shin Kwang Church, 1.9.2013; Dubai, Han-In Korean First Church, 20.9.2013

Text: II Corinthians 5:1

"For we know, that if the earthly frame that houses us today should be demolished, we possess a building which God has provided - - a house not made by human hands, eternal, and in heaven."

John 1: 6-9

"There appeared a man named John, sent from God; he came as a witness to testify to the light, that all might become believers through him. He was not himself the light; he came to bear witness to the light. The real light which enlightens every man was even then coming into the world."

The question of the existence or non-existence of a life after this life is a big question for most everyone. All humanity through all generations has been confronted with this issue of life and death. Because we know nothing or very little about it, it is of great concern to us. Some of you believe strongly in an afterlife, some do not believe at all and others are uncertain.

Today I would like to speak about this for three reasons: First, this question also interests me. Second, the Bible reveals much on this topic. Third, today science is examining this field, for example doctors, physicists, parapsychologists and others.

Let us begin with my own experiences. When I was about 26 years old, I gave little or no thought to this subject. If there was an existence after this life, that would be fine and if not that would be our destiny. All we have to do is live the best life on earth as we can. That was my thought.

One day in the summer of 1968 my mother said, "Saturday evening George Daisly will give a demonstration in the city auditorium in Anchorage. Our pastor Ralph Weeks recommends we go to this event. It is part of a revival or renewal movement here in the Anchorage area. Daisly comes from England but for many years has lived in Santa Barbara, California. He has psychic abilities and wants to introduce us to this world beyond. Would you like to come?"

Psychic phenomena have always fascinated me, so Saturday night we went with about 400 others. Mr. Daisly made several vivid presentations, which were all very amazing. Then he said, "I see several people in the audience with aureoles. I will try to read them". According to Daisly and scientists, all humans have aureoles around their bodies, which are all very different. An aureole or aura is a ring of electrical radiation in a magnetic field. They are of various colors, have different strengths and dissimilar wavelengths. Psychics with these special abilities can see them. Further, with scientific help anyone can see auras. We often define these auras as halos.

Because every radiation is different, Daisly could see in the auras the diverse personalities. Jesus had a strong aura with vivid colors. In John 12:46, Jesus says he is the light of the world. His aura of bright radiation is easily seen. Someone who is sensitive enough to see these phenomena is often also able to hear in the spiritual world. All this Daisly could do.

As a child, my spirituality began emerging and I started sensing or believing such things. On this evening I thought, "If all this really is true and if my feelings are right about myself then Daisly can also see and read my aura even though I am sitting rather far back in the auditorium". Suddenly he turned in my direction and amazingly, pointing to me, said, "Yes, you with the string tie". Indeed, he had seen my aura. Accurately he described some of my personality and a little of my past. Then he said, "I see a young man standing next to you, with his arm around your shoulder. He is a friend of yours about your same age and height. He was killed in a car accident about a year ago and sends his greetings to you". Daisly described perfectly my deceased friend Bill Betcher. Bill was killed while driving from Seward to Anchorage. I was amazed, because Daisly knew me not and I had never seen him! This medium introduced me to the world beyond and to my departed friend Bill.

Within the next three years, I spoke with George Daisly on six occasions. Two of these meetings were séances where I met people out of our earthly existence. One was my Norwegian grandfather, who always said, "Boy and boy!" to express amazement. I have never heard anyone use this expression except him. George Daisly spoke exactly these words from my grandfather. The correct American expression is, "Boy oh boy!" In addition, I was very astonished when Daisly told me, on one of these sittings, some of my future. Much of what he said has already occurred. Among other things, he said I would speak to many people in the German language and would speak to Asians. At that time, I had just graduated from seminary and had no thoughts about my future and I spoke no German. Since Daisly was so dogmatic about me speaking German, I was extremely puzzled. This fact was very difficult for me to believe. His comment about me speaking to Asians seemed to me as only a passing comment and I gave it little thought. Now, after having ministered 30 years to Swiss German churches, and after speaking 15 years in Korean churches, here I am again, talking to you: an Asian Korean community; — how illogical.

Of course, these experiences are no proof there is an afterlife but also no one can disprove an afterlife nor deny these spiritual experiences. I need no more evidence; my experiences and my biblical understandings confirm to me that there is a life after this one.

Further, it is extremely important to know that involving one's self with the supernatural world, as I did, can be very dangerous. Today I do not recommend such adventures; these escapades are no longer part of my life. The Holy Spirit protected me during these times. If someone by mistake does become involved with witchcraft, Shamanism or the like, leave this danger zone immediately. It can be deceiving and very risky! It is essential to ask for the Lord's protection. Insecure individuals and weak or gullible personalities should especially stay away from this gamble.

In 1970 while doing my master's degree at San Francisco Theological Seminary in San Anselmo, California and working at Covenant Presbyterian Church in Palo Alto, California, I had the opportunity to assist researchers in parapsychology at the well-known Stanford University where many years earlier Uri Geller was tested. Russell Targ, a physics researcher at Stanford was very skeptical when examining paranormal activities. Yet being very curious, he wanted to investigate this area in depth. At Stanford, scientists have researched this phenomenon studying many subjects and their astral-travel experiences. Some of these scientists have concluded that somehow the soul can separate from the body.

However, for Christians this is nothing new. The Bible has many texts supporting this phenomenon. When the spirit leaves the body, the body is dead but the spirit continues to live. In any case, many scientists have come to the conclusion, after measuring the electrical and magnetic impulses of the heart and brain, the soul can separate from the body.

One day while Russell and I were talking about the possibility of an afterlife he said, "I really don't want to believe it but I'm afraid that we must accept there is a future life". His conclusion had come from paranormal experiments and from interviewing people who described their strange experiences as their spirit and body had separated.

Several books describe such incidents. One is entitled, "Life After Life" by Raymond A. Moody, Jr., M.D. In his book he writes about 50 people he interviewed, who were clinically dead for a short time and had no hope of being reanimated.

The first report: (pp. 54-55)

"I was out of my body, there's no doubt about it, because I could see my own body there on the operating room table. My soul was out! All this made me feel very bad at first, but then, this really bright light came... It was tremendously bright; I just can't describe it. It seemed that it covered everything, yet it didn't prevent me from seeing everything around me - - the operating room, the doctors and nurses, everything. I could see clearly, and it wasn't blinding. I felt a warm sensation.

At first, when the light came, I wasn't sure what was happening, but then, it kind of asked me if I was ready to die. It was like talking to a person, but a person wasn't there. The light was talking to me, but in a voice."

My question:

What was this light? Did God speak? "I am the light of the world." Did this man meet Jesus?

Another account: (pp. 11-12)

"After a while, he collects himself and becomes more accustomed to his odd condition. He notices that he still has a 'body', but one of a very different nature and with very different powers from the physical body he has left behind. Soon other things begin to happen. Others come to meet and to help him. He glimpses the spirits of relatives and friends who have already died, and a loving, warm spirit of a kind he has never encountered before appears before him - - a being of light. This being asks him a question, nonverbally, to make him evaluate his life and helps him along by showing him a panoramic, instantaneous playback of the major events of his life."

My question:

Is this for him the "Judgment Day"?

"At some point he finds himself approaching some sort of barrier or border, apparently representing the limit between earthly life and the next life. Yet, he finds that he must go back to the earth, that the time for his death has not yet come. At this point he resists, for by now he is taken up with his experiences in the afterlife and does not want to return. He is overwhelmed by intense feelings of joy, love, and peace." (*This is exactly what God has promised us for the next life.)* "Despite his attitude, though, he somehow reunites with his physical body and lives."

A young woman relates this account: (p. 32)

"I thought I was dead, and I wasn't sorry that I was dead, but I just couldn't figure out where I was supposed to go. My thought and my consciousness were just like they are in life, but I just couldn't figure all this out. I kept thinking, "Where am I going to go? What am I going to do?" "My God, I'm dead! I can't believe it!"

Another report: (p. 18)

"Later I asked her what she remembered of her "death". She said she didn't remember much about it, except that she did hear me say, "Let's try one more time and then we'll give up." The doctor did say exactly these words.

A woman told this: (p.46)

"I realized that all these people were there, almost in multitudes it seemed, hovering around the ceiling of the room. They were all people I had known in my past life, but who had passed on before. I recognized my grandmother and a girl I had known when I was in school, and many other relatives and friends. It seems that I mainly saw their faces and felt their presence. They all seemed pleased. It was a very happy occasion, and I felt that they had come to protect or to guide me."

Finally a soldier in Vietnam reported: (pp. 62-63)

"At the point of impact (when I was shot), my life began to become a picture in front of me, and it seemed that I could go back to the time when I was still a baby, and the pictures seemed to progress through my whole life.

I could remember everything; everything was so vivid. It was so clear in front of me. It shot right by me, from the earliest things I can remember right on up to the present, and it all happened within a short time. And it was not anything bad at all. I went through it with no regrets, no derogatory feelings about myself at all."

Dear friends, also in the time of Paul the Apostle there were people who had similar experiences as those of some today. One of Paul's many and clearest texts about heaven is our sermon text: "For we know, that if the earthly frame, that houses us today, should be demolished, we possess a building which God has provided - - a house not made by human hands, eternal, and in heaven."

What I have spoken about today may seem strange to some of you but many people have had these experiences. All these reports correspond with each other in some way making it difficult to discount them. However, if one has not had a similar experience it is not always easy to accept the experiences of others.

Nevertheless, I am sure there are those in our presence who have something comparable to tell. At any rate, this is something about which we can think. In addition to Biblical history, my experiences have confirmed my belief in a spiritual non-earthly life after our worldly existence. One might say, my paranormal experiences (the back door) have confirmed my Biblical belief in an afterlife (the front door being the Bible)!

In conclusion, we read again Paul's text for today:

"For we know, that if the earthly frame, that houses us today, should be demolished, we possess a building which God has provided - - a house, not made by human hands, eternal, and in heaven."

Prayer: Let us pray.

Dear Lord open us, so we can feel your presence. Let us be sensitive to the truth about life and death. Help us to know what we need to know about our future. We will never know all the answers and secrets until we pass through the door which continues into our future existence. Again, dear Lord guide us in our thoughts and knowledge about our non-earthly journey when we live as spirits. Let us know, after we leave our material bodies, that we need have no fear of our unknown future reality.
In Jesus' Name, AMEN.

Benediction:

May the Lord bless us and keep us,
May the Lord let his face shine upon us,
and be gracious unto us,
May the Lord lift up his countenance upon us,
and give us peace until we meet again.
In the name of Jesus Christ, our Lord. Amen.

Book Reference:

"Jeder hat den 6. Sinn: Neue Erkenntnisse über die Psychischen des Menschen"
von Targ Russell / Puthoff Harold

Thanksgiving When I don't Feel Thankful

Thanksgiving Sermon

Seong Nam, Shin Kwang Church, 19.11.2006

Scripture: Psalms 28:6-9

Text: II Corinthians 9:10-15; (Luke 12:22-31)

Three weeks ago we celebrated here in Shin Kwang Church "Chuseok" (추석) your Korean harvest festival. Today is Thanksgiving in the USA, our harvest festival. The first settlers in America were also thankful for good crops.

Boom – Thanksgiving – here it is again, – now we must all be thankful! However, if I have an ungrateful disposition on this special day and am not thankful, how can I be thankful? Today might be a day when nothing is going right. All my hopes and dreams are shattered and now it is easier to see all my frustrations rather than my pleasures. If I am irritated with everything and everybody around me, how can I be thankful? I want to complain when listening to the news; if I could be in charge, it would be a better world. Maybe my arthritis is bad and even worsening. At such times, I would rather complain than be thankful and sing hymns of admiration.

How would it be, if we would make an annual Complaingiving Day? We could discharge all our gripes and grievances and as Shakespeare said, "Cleanse the stuffed bosom of that perilous stuff which weighs upon the heart". The advantage of this would be 364 days of thankfulness. Now, some might think, we give thanks once a year and have 364 days to grumble and complain.

This of course is nonsense, since Thanksgiving should be a time to remind us of the riches we receive every day of our lives. We receive from our ancestors, from our families and friends, and from many people we will never see or know. People provide us with food, hospitals and protection, with books, machines and artwork, and with entertainment and intellectual nourishment.

On Thanksgiving Day we can be thankful for all this, just as we are thankful on birthdays, Christmas or Easter when we remember our loved ones. We do not celebrate parent's day in order to forget them the rest of the year. Neither should Thanksgiving free us from continually thanking God.

How can I be thankful when I am not thankful, even if I was taught I should always be thankful? How can I switch on a lever to make me feel thankful, if I am dejected, or irritable? Since we do not live in a world where everyone has the awesome attitude of giving thanks, how can we be thankful? There is much fear in our world of violence. We are angry toward some of our leaders and leaders of other countries, and terrorism continually confronts us. Thus, this morning I want to speak about "How to be thankful when I don't feel thankful". How can I be thankful when so many people around us really do live in difficult situations with hunger, war and cruelty?

I think we have all experienced "discipline". It is something that we probably do not always like to practice. However, it has always been a part of all civilizations. In Korea, hierarchy is a very strong part of the culture. Consequently, discipline is also experienced to a high degree here, more so than in many western countries.

I think and hope most of you have come to church today willingly and happily. Nevertheless, some of you would not be here unless you had developed what I call the "discipline of worship". A Christian believer or church member is one who accepts the "discipline of worship".

We live in a time when the emphasis is frequently on our "feelings". What are you feeling now? What is your emotional state? A number of years ago there was much talk about the human race having "come of age". One might say we have reentered childhood (I want what I want when I want it!). We hear children say, "I don't feel like eating my spinach." "I don't feel like going to school today." "Why should I visit Grandpa, if I don't feel like it?" Not many parents appreciate such excuses. Yet adults often say exactly the same things. We say to ourselves, "I don't feel like writing that letter." "I don't feel like visiting my parents on this special parent's day." "I don't feel like attending church today." "I don't feel like going to the cemetery on this Chuseok."

For Non-Koreans, "Chuseok" is not only a harvest festival but it is also set aside for families to visit there deceased relatives at the cemetery.

Sometimes I do not feel like singing a hymn early Sunday morning in church. However, here I discover how that word "discipline" begins to help me. I notice, by the time I have sung the hymn, I am already feeling better, more genuinely thankful and grateful to God, more ready to start the day in a spirit of thankfulness. I am sure I am speaking to some of you too, who have had this experience. Perhaps it has already happened to you in this service. The discipline of worship brings its own reward.

Let me confess, I do not like sitting upstairs in the balcony in a Shin Kwang Church service, where I cannot see what is happening at the pulpit, or on the stage. When I sit behind a big head of hair, in the back row of the gallery, I cannot even see the Pastor! If I understood the language – okay, that might be better! Is this discipline for me – not seeing, or understanding, and still worshiping? Should I discipline myself and listen, or should I shut my eyes and sleep while others worship? All joking aside, I must always remember I am fortunate. Not everyone has the opportunity to sit in church as I can! I also know, when just being in church, I experience fellowship with other Christians and can feel the presence of the Holy Spirit. This is also important. If we all developed the habit of saying to ourselves, as we get out of bed each morning, "Thank you God!" I trust we would probably be able to overcome the gloominess of those low-spirited and thankless days. Maybe we would feel better if we opened the drapes and let the sun shine in our room and say, "Glory is to the Father, and to the Son, and to the Holy Spirit!"

In addition, there is this mystery of our shared lives as Christians, the fellowship, the love, or koinonia (Christian fellowship) of the Church. We might call it the working of the Holy Spirit, who makes us thankful for our lives and our relationships.

We can contaminate Thanksgiving with negative thoughts and actions just as we can poison pessimism, and depression, with positive thoughts and actions. It is part of our commitment as Christians to be willing to open our souls and minds to praise and worship in the Church. We have no right to isolate ourselves from giving thanks as worshipers in a living church.

It should not be possible to sit crouched in our secluded misery, when the praise and love of the Church is all around us. When I hear someone say, "I feel better after I've been to church", I think churchgoers partially mean the following. On a big day of celebration, such as Thanksgiving, Christmas or Easter, it might just happen that some special hardship has come to us perhaps illness, bad news, or death. I trust at this time, we are uplifted by the faith, gratitude and love of our fellow-believers. Now we are able to know the grace and beauty of a grateful soul, even when there seems so little in which to rejoice. We can experience the warmth of good spirits next to us. It takes just a few truly thankful people to change the climate of a whole community.

There is another thought which could also encourage us to sing and be thankful when we do not feel like it. However, sadly, it is not a very real part of our Christianity. A biblical understanding is, "Rejoice with those, who rejoice, and weep with those, who weep". It is thought provoking, that we are far more responsive to the second half. We learn as Christians our responsibility is to empathize with neighbors in their dilemmas, to offer comfort to the saddened and try to remove their grief, "to weep with those, who weep". However, how often do we think it is necessary "to rejoice with those who rejoice"? This is a more difficult Christian kindness to practice. When things are fine with us, it is not hard to show compassion with those in misery. Nevertheless, when we are suffering, we need special strength to enter genuinely into the joys of others. "I don't feel like giving thanks" we say to ourselves, when asked to rejoice in the celebration of a marriage, or baptism, if we ourselves are sad, or distressed. However, the Bible says, "We can be happy when we are sad". If we try, we can experience Christianity in ourselves when we give thanks; giving thanks does not depend on our feelings. It is possible to be thankful when we are sad, miserable, depressed, or even angry. God, the Holy Spirit, will help us. Thanksgiving is sharing with others the mutual, eternal gratefulness we have for God's gifts of love, and for his Good News.

When we "don't feel like thanking", it is good to remember, there is no situation which should stop us from being thankful for our creation, for our security and for our blessings. Over many generations and in countless cultures men and women have often undergone poverties, hazards and distresses, and have even then given many words of thanks. The American Pilgrims, at the beginning of their history in 1621, repeated words of thanks. These men and women struggled in times of hardships in a new and strange land, through cold winters and frequently with hostile Indians.

We think of this country and those suffering during the Japanese occupation in Korea, between 1910 and 1945. We think of families struck by unpredictable and fatal diseases, the tragedy of the "comfort women", and the agony of hunger and the loss of life. Despite this anguish, those brave people also prayed words of thanks. All these men and women have said in very difficult times, "We thank you God for our creation, protection, and for all the blessings you have given us." In the face of this witness, how can we, as prosperous and advantaged people, living in a free country, with few worries as compared to other parts of the world, utter these disgraceful words: "I don't feel like being thankful"?

We have the fortune of living in a country, where a special time is dedicated to giving thanks to God. This month we also celebrate Thanksgiving in Switzerland, "Erntedankfest".

May the spirit of this season generate such a sense of gratitude in our hearts, that in the year ahead, morning, noon, and night, "in plenty and in want; in joy and in sorrow; in sickness and in health" we will always give thanks to God. AMEN.

Thank God for Suffering

Seong Nam; Shin Kwang Church, 18.11.2007

Texts: Jeremiah 17:5-10; John 10:7-18

Some of you like to close your eyes in church! Are you sleeping or just resting your eyes?! I confess, sometimes I shut my eyes in church too. Today I want you to close your eyes! I have something important to say but you do not need to see me! You only need your ears and imagination.

Close your eyes now. With closed eyes, paint a picture in your mind of a beautiful or peaceful scene where you would like to be. It could be in an open field, in a picturesque forest by a gentle stream or maybe at "Seoraksan" (설악산). It could also be in another country or it might be in your home with family and friends. If it is not a pleasant scene, paint the unpleasantness you imagine. All pictures are good because all pictures depict different areas and times of life. Life has many good parts but sadly also contains painful segments, unhappy events, even dreadful things.
(Two minute pause)

Keep your eyes closed and use all the colors necessary to give your picture the trueness of life. If your scene is sad, dreary or unpleasant you might use dark colors and if it is a happy image, you could use bright colors. With closed eyes, take your time as you paint your picture. I will give you a minute or two more to paint.
(Two more minutes of silence)

Keep your eyes closed and draw yourself into this picture. Try to portray all the facial expressions that show your feelings. In this picture where are you and what are you doing? How do you feel? I will continue to give you another two minutes of silence.
(Continue pause)

Keep your eyes closed.

Maybe you have painted a picture of a joyous, happy moment. Maybe it is from the past or present. It could also be another picture from your imagination, maybe something in the future. Perhaps you have painted a sad, dreary, or painful image. Whatever the scene is, look at what you have painted. Look at all the parts of the picture and make your observations. Look at yourself and see how you appear in the scene. What does this picture mean to you? Keep your eyes closed and I will give you more time for self-reflection.
(Continue pause)

Now open your eyes.

The Hebrew people in the Old Testament painted pictures similar to what you have just drawn. They tried to understand themselves in relationship to the land around them. Land depicted a great deal in Hebrew thinking. The land and its conditions meant their survival or death, thus they often made land images. The earth under their feet was their most precious possession because they lived from the soil. They cultivated crops on it, raised sheep and cattle, and found drinking water there. Hebrew people were very close to the earth and actually became identified with it.

Jeremiah writes in Chapter 17, 5-8:

5. The Lord says, "Cursed is the one who trusts in man, who depends on flesh for his strength, and whose heart turns away from the Lord.

6. He will be like a bush in the wastelands; he will dwell in the parched places of the desert, in a salt land, where no one lives.

7. But blessed is the man, who trusts in the Lord, whose confidence is in him.

8. He will be like a tree planted by the water that sends out its roots by the stream. It does not fear, when heat comes; its leaves are always green. It has no worries in a year of drought and never fails to bear fruit."

Here are two environments painted by Jeremiah. One is the salt land and parched desert. The other is a land with meadows, trees and streams. We can live in either a parched desert or a green meadow, but there is only one satisfying place for us to live. We cannot enjoy and be happy in a good and beautiful land unless we have experienced the dried up, unwanted fields and a barren terrain. The land of meadows, trees, and streams becomes holy if we are experiencing life in a desert wasteland. This contrast, which Jeremiah makes, enables us to appreciate and understand what is beautiful.

Now look at your own painting again. What you drew is meaningful and valuable. If it is a happy picture, you can enjoy it more after you have seen a sad or hostile picture, or one with pain and suffering.

Through a picture of cursedness, we become aware and thoughtful of who we are and what we have in life. We learn to value our life and find reasons for rejoicing in its beauty after we have seen life's dark side.

If we are sick, depressed or unhealthy in some way, or if we are hospitalized we may think we are only enduring a hardship in a desolate, cursed wasteland. Conversely, it is not an inhospitable desert wilderness. Even a desert is full of life. It is true nevertheless, when living in a strange and barren land we suffer, since it is unfamiliar to our normal enjoyable lifestyle. Yet this suffering is good! It allows us to become aware and passionate about our life of happiness when all is going well. We may forget to value life's good side if we only experience happiness and luxury. Often we take this good part of life for granted. We do not appreciate our prosperity, joyfulness, and health.

Further, if we only know the good side of life, we might think we are experiencing life's bad side, since we have never known the bad side of life, when in fact, life's good side is good. For example, Hanwan enjoys his favourite bibimbap. Later he eats bullgogi. The bullgogi then is tasteless for him, since he has only eaten food he prefers. This is unfortunate, since both bibimbap and bullgogi are equally tasteful. Additionally, if we have only enjoyed the positive we can never understand those suffering the negative. Since we have only experienced the positive, we think the negative, they are experiencing, must also be positive. Consequently, we can truly thank God when he lets us experience the negative. Only after we have gone through "the valley of the shadow of death" (Psalm 23:4) are we able to enjoy and appreciate life's good side. We must know, "the Lord remembers us and blesses us" (Psalm 115:12).

If now you are enduring the dreadful, you must know without this dreadful you cannot enjoy happiness. Because we thank God for letting us experience terrible times we also need to ask him to give us strength and courage to be able to endure these troubles and hardships. We know God remembers us and blesses us. We can also thank him for the goodness in life.

According to Jeremiah, it is not the actual existence of the good land with green pastures, young trees and fresh water, which gives us happiness. Instead, the land of pastures, trees, and streams is comparable with someone who trusts in God even though he has problems and difficulties. This trusting is the way we will find happiness and a good rewarding life. We want to trust God for he has a special life for all of us, a meaningful and useful life even when we experience life's incomprehensible wasteland.

Yet, not all is wasteland. We can become like the young trees, running water and green fields. We must know however, God's plan for us does include suffering. There is a reason for all suffering and suffering is not in vain.

Jesus never said we would not suffer. He said, "I am the gate; whoever enters through me will be saved. He will come in and go out and find pasture." (John 10:9) This means even though we will suffer on earth we can enter through Jesus' door which includes misery and be rescued from danger, harm and damnation. By going through the gate, accepting our suffering, we demonstrate our faith and trust in God. By asking him for help as we go through the trials and tribulations of life, we show our belief. We are able to thank God for happiness as well as suffering.

How do you respond to suffering? Do you go through God's gate letting yourself not only acknowledge pleasure but also accept misery? It is easy to say "yes" I will go through the gate, but do you really go through it accepting what God has in store for you, both pleasure and suffering? You can fool yourself, but you cannot fool God. Are you honest with yourself and God?

The message of hope, truth and joy that Jeremiah gave his people completes his picture. This is Jesus' message and can likewise complete our picture. In him, we find hope, truth, and joy. Jesus is our example to follow. He is the way of life, the way of love and the way of peace. We experience this message when we go through his gate letting him guide us through pleasures and hardships.

Prayer: Let us pray:

Lord thank you for letting us suffer hardships, sadness and problems. We know without suffering we cannot know the joys and good things in life. Nevertheless, suffering is very difficult for us. Give us the strength and courage to be able to endure suffering, to live with it and to value it as part of your good life's plan for us. We know you only want the best for us even if we do not understand your methods, even though we do not know why you let us suffer. We want to trust and have faith in you despite all of life's seemingly unbearable hardships. God, we know that when we live according to your will we can experience the joy and happiness of life about which you teach. Lord, be with us always. Give us strength when we are weak so we can do what is right. In Jesus' name, Amen.

Jesus said: "I am the light of the world; he who follows me will not walk in darkness, but will have the light of life." (John 8:12b)

Benediction:

Let God's love and peace be with all of you.
May you find the light about which Jesus teaches.

Comparing Swiss and Korean Churches: Don't judge Others

Sang Nam, Addressed at the Seoul Annual Regional Ecumenical Conference, 19.5.2006

Text: Matthew 7:1-2

I would like to thank you for giving me this opportunity to speak to you at this conference. I bring greetings from the Evangelical Reformed Church of Switzerland and from my former church in Ostermundigen, a community adjacent to the city of Bern. The city of Bern is the capital of Switzerland and is the capital of the state or Canton of Bern. Switzerland has 26 cantons, and a population of about 7 ½ million.

Today I would like to talk about the Swiss Evangelical Reformed Church and compare it in a small way to the Christian church in Korea.

All Christians, even non-confessing Christians, are born into a state church if their parents are members. Thus, we have many Swiss Christians, most are however so-called "paper Christians" or in today's world, I call them "computer Christians". In other words, they are in our files but they rarely or never attend church. The three state churches are the Reformed or Protestant Church, the Roman Catholic Church, and the Christ Catholic Church. The Christ Catholic Church is similar to the Episcopal Church in the USA, or the Anglican Church in England.

The population of Ostermundigen is about 16,000 and about 8000 are members of the Reformed tradition. The rest belong to the Catholic Church, other Christian denominations and a small percentage belongs to various religions such as Buddhism, Hinduism and Islam or they belong to no church. On a normal Sunday there are between 75 and 100 worshipers who attend the Reformed Church in Ostermundigen. About 1.25% of the church members attend regularly. This sounds like a small percent, but we must consider several things. Korean Christianity is very young. One is not born into the Korean church; he must join. Almost everyone is born into the Christian Church in Switzerland. Since Koreans join their Church, it is clear there is a higher percentage of Christians attending their Sunday services. In Korea, Sunday church attendance appears more important than in Switzerland. Swiss consider other church activities just as important and sometimes even more essential. The population of the city of Seoul alone is over 10 million inhabitants considerably larger than the entire country of Switzerland. In Korea, about 18% of Protestant Christians attend Sunday church regularly and less than 2% of Swiss Protestant members attend frequently.

Some Swiss church activities include hiking, skiing, discussion groups on many topics, sacred dancing, and other family and adult events. Prayer meetings, Bible classes, mother/children circles, groups for distributing food and clothes to the poor, fund raising bazaars, public forums, and German classes for refugees, church cultural activities including concerts and plays, as well as other happenings, are common.

The percentage of active Christians is probably about the same in Switzerland as in Korea. Unfortunately, both Swiss and Korean church membership is declining.

It is interesting that all Swiss church members, including non-confessing computer Christians, desire the church's services. Here are some recent annual statistics for the Canton of Bern: there are about 1450 weddings, 4480 baptisms, 6500 confirmations, 7200 funerals, 270 new members, and 3150 "Computer Christians" who ended their church membership. Bern is the largest canton in Switzerland. It has about 375 reformed churches, with more than 600,000 members.

Theologically, the Swiss Reformed Church is identical to the Presbyterian churchs in the USA. These churches can be liberal, conservative, or rudimentary. The rudimentary Christians, often called "fundamental" Christians interpret the Bible strictly and literally. The Evangelical Reformed Church of Switzerland tends to be liberal, with exceptions, and has fewer liturgies than USA Presbyterian churches. The Presbyterian Church of Korea (PCK) is generally conservative with fundamental tendencies. The Korean Full Gospel Church (Assembly of God) is fundamental. Korean church liturgy is similar to American Presbyterian liturgy.

It is impossible to compare Swiss with Korean churches for several reasons. Roman Catholic Christian Missionaries came to Korea from the USA about 225 years ago and taught Catholicism in this non-Christian country. About 125 years ago, Protestant Christian Missionaries also came to Korea from the USA and taught the traditional rudimentary Reformed tradition. Western Christianity, on the other hand, is almost 2000 years old.

When I use the term "Christianity" I mean both Roman Catholic and Protestant Christians. Sometimes Korean Catholic Christians do not consider Protestant Christians to be true Christians. Protestants sometimes think of Catholics in the same way as not being true Believers. Other Christian denominations frequently think their values are the only true ones.

We have many ecumenical activities intertwining Protestant, Catholic and other denominations. We learn from each other through mutual events such as church services, bazars, senior citizen afternoons, adult and youth Bible study classes, and other joint church functions.

The Reformation in Europe occurred more than 450 years ago, and about 50 or 60 years ago, a new movement began. I call it the "New Reformation".

On Feb. 7, 1528, the Reformation began in the Canton of Bern. The Protestants separated from the recognized Roman Catholic Church resulting in many dreadful actions in the name of Christianity. Even today, Rome considers Protestants as second class Christians. Fortunately, outside of Rome, progress is being made and we are experiencing throughout the western world this "New Reformation" — the "Ecumenical Movement". Both churches are beginning to accept each other.

In addition, because of our different cultures, a comparison between Swiss and Korean churches is impossible. Korean Christians are Christian in their heads, Buddhist in their hearts, Shaman in their stomachs and Confucian in their feet, the history on which they stand. Western Christians are Christian in their heads, hearts, stomachs, and feet. They only know Christianity.

When American missionaries came to Korea they brought with them conservative and fundamental Christianity. This is generally very spiritual, and/or supernatural. Some of these Christians spoke in tongues, healed the sick, and did other miracles. Sometimes they even did uncanny things such as casting out evil spirits, which still occurs sometimes today.

For Korean Christians it is often easier to accept the mystical in Christianity than it is for many western Christians. This is largely due to Korea's history of shamanism.

In Switzerland, many members are leaving the state churches partially because church members are often materialistic and scientific, and want proof. Obviously, the supernatural cannot be proven. Spirituality, and God's working, can only be experienced. This non-belief without proof hinders spirituality in the churches. Because these people cannot find proof, they cannot believe, thus they are unable to have, or to recognize spiritual experiences, and then they leave the church.

Often however, some members leave a liberal church in order to join a conservative or fundamental church, where spirituality is more often observed in its members and practiced by them. This can be positive but it can also be dangerous. In such churches, new members may experience spirituality easier, however on rare occasions fundamental churches can lead some Christians into sorcery or witchcraft without the church realizing what it is doing.

In addition, such fundamental churches tell their members what they must believe and do, in order to enter God's kingdom. If members obey the church's instructions they go to heaven and if not they go to hell! To obey is easier than to think. Often lazy or comfortable believers join such churches. On the other hand, liberal churches do not threaten its members with heaven and hell, are not legalistic and things are less black and white. Thus, one has to think for himself, decide what is right, and then have faith and courage to do it, which is often difficult. Sometimes a person leaves the church because he thinks he must believe according to certain basic biblical teachings. If he cannot accept these strict fundamental traditions, he says he is not a Christian, thus he leaves the church. This is especially true if a person has been raised in one of these strict churches. The more liberal church believes there is more than one way to enter God's kingdom.

Another reason for one leaving the church is so that he does not have to pay the annually required and automatically deducted church taxes. Some leave for political reasons or out of disinterest. Interest is lost when a church cannot challenge its members or give them answers they can use.

In the 1970's Korean Church membership increased rapidly. In the following years, membership stagnated. In the late 1990's until now church affiliation has been declining. Also in Korea, church members have not always received needed answers. When the church cannot give usable answers or challenge its members, Christian faith stagnates and church membership decreases. Since Christianity is young in Korea, worshipers are unable to ask pertinent theological questions. They only know the one Biblical theology, which they have been taught thus are unable to consider other possibilities.

One lady said, when asked why she left the Korean Church, "I cannot learn anything new and I do not think the pastors can answer my questions, maybe they do not want to give answers. Anyway it is hard for me to ask him questions."

Pastors cannot be doubted. Korean culture and tradition says nonprofessionals should not question authorities. Thus, some Koreans are polite, do not ask questions, remain uninformed and leave the church! Westerners are not only allowed and encouraged to ask questions but it is accepted. Sometimes it is expected that believers question their superiors. By asking questions, one learns and teaches!

Swiss Christians do not pray as often in public as do Koreans. I pray with my eyes open, walking down the street, standing in the rain, riding a bicycle or walking in the forest. When admiring the nature and its beauty I am praying and thanking God. The way I relate to my fellowman can also be a prayer. I try to make my life a prayer. Often people do not know when I am praying.

The Korean Church is in some ways naive. Koreans do not have to prove their Christianity, as often do westerners. This is good. The Bible says, "Believe as a child". It is often easier to experience the spiritual in the Korean's non-proof Christianity. Though my theology differs in some ways from Korean theology, I feel the Christian atmosphere often more here than in my church. Nevertheless, sometimes a Korean goes to church to show others he is Christian or for other political reasons. Once I experienced this in Sang Nam just before an election when a presidential candidate suddenly appeared in church. Another time I observed an active Roman Catholic Christian unexpectedly in our protestant church in Anchorage. He was a candidate for the governor's office in Alaska. He had never attended our Presbyterian church, but just before the election, he appeared at our Sunday service. He did win the election, as did the Sang Nam presidential candidate!

Sometimes we judge other Christians. As mentioned earlier maybe Protestants do not consider Catholics to be true Christians, or vice versa. Also maybe fundamentals do not consider liberals to be true Christians or vice versa. Some think, “Only my church has the truth”. However, we are all Christians and we can only believe as we believe. Christians in different countries believe differently because of their individual histories and cultures, and because of their different personalities and types of intelligences. It would be impossible for all Christians to believe alike and if they did, it would be very uninteresting. There would be no theological discussions between Christians. We all should be able to attend the same church and absorb from our different beliefs.

Though different Christian denominations have different theological philosophies we are all Christians. We confess our basic Christian faith when we say the “Apostles Creed” together. I think it is important that we all learn from each other.

Our sermon text says, “Do not judge others”. Let us remember this.

Though we cannot really compare Swiss and Korean churches, there are some parallels. I have not considered all the aspects on this subject and some things I have said will require discussion. Furthermore, if I have made any false assumptions about your Korean churches or traditions please correct me.

I think I can give you new theological ideas and you can help me in my Christian life.

In my living and working in Korea I have gotten to know, understand, value and love you in many ways. You have a beautiful country and a very special Christianity. Thank you for listening.

A Child's Question

Seong Nam, Shin Kwang Church, 14.05.2006; ….., Joongang Dandae Church, 25.05 2008

Children's Day/Parent's Day/Mother's Day Sermon

Text: Luke 2:41-50

This month we celebrated Children's Day and Parent's Day. Therefore, I want to comment on children's questions to God and parent's reactions to their questions.

Jesus had many questions as a child. One time he disappeared for three long days to get some answers. He was gone from his parents without their knowledge. Naturally, they were quite worried about his absence and unhappy that he had not told them where he was going. When they found him in the temple with famous teachers asking many questions, they were greatly amazed and astonished about his understanding. Jesus did not go to Mary and Joseph with his questions maybe because he thought his parents would not have answers. Perhaps they were little concerned or too busy for his seemingly unimportant questions. He went to the temple to find answers probably for several reasons.

In any case, when Jesus was a boy he wondered about many things as do children and young people today. How do we respond when a young person comes to us with a question about God? Do we ignore him because we do not know the answer, or are we unconcerned? Are we too busy for seemingly trivial questions? Whatever the reason may be, youth sometimes turn away from Christianity because they do not receive satisfactory answers. Surprisingly when we seriously consider some of the questions children ask they are really quite profound.

Here are two such examples found in a book called "Children's Letters to God":

> Dear God, I have got to know something. What is it like in Heaven? I know it's nice, but what kind of nice? What happens when it rains?
> Marty

A second letter to God.

> Dear God, what is it like when you die? Nobody will tell me. I just want to know. I don't want to do it.
> Your friend, Mike

Here is an appropriate question from another child. I found it in one of John Updike's short stories entitled "Pigeon Feathers". David had again come home from a Sunday school class disillusioned. He had become hardened because he thought he and Christianity had been betrayed.

Here is David's conversation with his mother:

> "I asked Rev. Dobson about Heaven and he said it was like Abraham Lincoln's goodness living after him." He waited for the shock to strike her.
> "Yes?" she said, expecting more. "That's all. And why didn't you like it?"
> "Well, don't you see? It amounts to saying there isn't any heaven at all."
> "I don't see that it amounts to that. What do you want Heaven to be?"
> "Well, I don't know. I want it to be something. I thought he'd tell me what it was. I thought it was his job."

He was becoming angry sensing her surprise at him. She assumed that Heaven had vanished from his head years ago. She had imagined that he had already entered into the secrecy of silence, which he knew to be all around him.

Yes, adults often underestimate the importance of a child's question. Answers are often too complicated or too simple for children, or they are in some other way insufficient. Maybe the answers do not fit our time or fit the child's situation.

In this excerpt, Mother is unaware of the importance of David's question. She assumes he is not troubled with such questions. Her concerns are not the same as his. She does not realize that his questions are just as important for him, as her concerns are for her.

For example, a child is concerned about a toy; a teenager, about a boyfriend or a girlfriend; a mother is concerned about the dinner; and a father, about his job and money. All are very important issues for each person involved.

Yes, even parents have questions many of which are kept secret because parents think their questions might be childish. Some say adults should not have childish questions. No questions are childish. All inquiries are vital for the one asking them.

Often we do not give children answers because we ourselves are uncertain, confused or embarrassed about our answers. Therefore, we evade their questions. Even though at times it is difficult to discuss certain topics, a parent is being unfair and insincere with his child if he or she does not at least try to talk with the child about his requests. Further, there is nothing wrong with letting a child know that even you do not have answers to all questions.

David as well as all children and Jesus too have and have had profound questions about life. Many of these questions are not related or not directly related to religion. In any case, as parents and Christians it is our job and responsibility to deal with these issues.

Certainly, we need not expect our children to ask philosophical questions and study in temples as Jesus did. Neither should we expect them to ask the same questions and develop profound answers. However, it would be wise for parents to expect theological inquiries from their children and not make light of them or ignore them. A parent may legitimately ask how he can answer some of the questions his children ask. There are no easy solutions. Even pastors do not have all the answers. We can learn much about God but we will never know all God's mysteries. Therefore, Sören Kierkegaard, a well-known Danish philosopher and theologian, called God the "Unknown".

If we find no answer or solution to a child's question, where do we go? How can our human questions be answered? The answer is easy: Teach your children to pray, to read the Bible, to compare the biblical past with the modern present, to read many books, to examine and change their lives for the better, and to love their neighbors as themselves. Then they would have a strong faith and all their questions would be answered!

No, no, no, no, that is all wrong! How does all that nonsense help a child when he has no idea what he should do to accomplish this unrealistic and inhuman task? Yes, these are good answers but achieving them is far from reality. How then can we make a beginning? In some way, we have to hear God when he speaks. When God speaks, we must truly listen. God does not always speak when we wish. We must always be listening for God, which is most of the time not easy.

Now let us go back to the child-parent relationship. Let me try to give you a few suggestions on how we can understand a child and begin to answer his questions. In doing this however it often takes patience from parents and children.

First, from early childhood it is important to read and discuss Bible stories together with children. For small children as well as for every age group there are good books and Bibles, which are well illustrated and interesting. Both children and adults can be satisfied with these books and Biblical interpretations. We should find a regular time for Bible reading, remembering that answers do not always come in a few days or weeks. Maybe it takes years or a lifetime.

Second, adults should not try to hide their questions. Parents have to be clear and honest in their discussions. Children can also help clarify difficult questions by asking questions. Honesty and openness with children are extremely important. Children often know when we keep secrets from them and they do not appreciate it. The more children love us the more we are their examples. When parents keep secrets, children think secrets are okay, so they also will not tell their parents everything. Parents and children are then untruthful with each other.

Third, we must take our children seriously. We want the same from them. They often suspect us, when we are not genuine and sincere with them.

Fourth, I have already mentioned prayer, which is also important. We can pray everywhere even during a learning process. We may pray that we understand the Bible, that we are sensitive and aware of our lives, that we are open and straightforward with ourselves, our children and with God. When we hear God's answer and respond positively to it we can expect to understand life more fully. Then when we understand our personal lives understanding our children will also be improved, thus making children's questions easier to manage and answer.

Through prayer, we may also expect to be enlightened in ways we never expected. Responding positively to God also means we will want to serve our children and our fellowman. In serving those around us, we will be doing God's will.

We read in James 1, 5-6:

"If any of you lacks wisdom, let him ask God, who gives to all men generously, and without reproaching, and it will be given him. But let him ask in faith, with no doubting, for he who doubts is like a wave of the sea that is driven and tossed by the wind."

We can study, learn and have knowledge but without prayer many of the important questions about life cannot be answered. We have to take what Kierkegaard calls "the leap of faith". That is, we have to leap into the unknown. We have to take a step further. We have to go where we are unsure and do the uncertain. We must fully trust God.

We may ask how we can take "the leap of faith". Well, it certainly does not mean to jump from a cliff out into the sky and have faith that you will land safely, that is unless you have a parachute or delta glider!

Instead, we must act according to our conscience and respond in the way we understand God is leading our lives. When we try our best to live according to Jesus' example we can expect to experience many good things in life. Even if all our questions are not answered with certainty we can be reassured that with God's help and compassion we will gain knowledge in many of life's secrets. We will not always receive "yes" or "no" answers, but that does not mean we will not find the answers. As I said, we may have to wait a long time, but responses will come.

We may discover that earlier asked questions are no longer relevant for our Christian lives. We may find it is not necessary to prove everything, which of course is not possible. Some questions may be answered precisely because they will not be answered.

We must not forget "the leap of faith" means to trust God and to do what Jesus taught us, which means to live for those around us. Especially important is that we nurture our children and be responsible for their upbringing and well-being. Taking "the leap of faith" could be very difficult, but exactly that is our task and our responsibility as parents and Christians. We should realize our children are our most precious treasures. We are responsible for their happiness and welfare, for loving them and for answering their questions. With sincere prayer, we can expect God's help.

Prayer:

Dear God, we thank you for the opportunity to learn in your world. Open us to your teachings so that we can be prepared for tomorrow. We know we can receive answers to the important questions of life only when we have faith in you and respond positively to you. Only when we take a step into the unknown, only when we risk giving ourselves, and only if we try to live according to your wishes can we expect to obtain the vital answers of life. Help us to trust you and follow your teachings. Give parents wisdom to be able to understand their children and be patient with them. Be with all children and give them insight as they grow into responsible adults. Be with parents and children when they are with each other and talking to each other. In Jesus' name, Amen.

Love is Accepting

Seong Nam, Shin Kwang Church, 20.04.08

Youth Sermon

Scripture: Mathew 25, 14-30

Text: Acts 3, 1-10

1 Now Peter and John were going up to the temple at the hour of prayer, the ninth hour.
2 And a man lame from birth was being carried, whom they laid daily at the gate of the temple that is called the Beautiful Gate to ask alms of those entering the temple.
3 Seeing Peter and John about to go into the temple, he asked to receive alms.
4 And Peter directed his gaze at him, as did John, and said, "Look at us."
5 And he fixed his attention on them, expecting to receive something from them.
6 But Peter said, "I have no silver and gold, but what I do have I give to you. In the name of Jesus Christ of Nazareth, rise up and walk!"
7 And he took him by the right hand and raised him up, and immediately his feet and ankles were made strong.
8 And leaping up he stood and began to walk, and entered the temple with them, walking and leaping and praising God.
9 And all the people saw him walking and praising God,
10 and recognized him as the one who sat at the Beautiful Gate of the temple, asking for alms. And they were filled with wonder and amazement at what had happened to him.

Imagine what the almsman thought when Peter and John came to him and said they had no silver or gold. After all, he was sitting there by the temple gate asking for money in order for him to make his meager existence. He must have thought, "Who do you think you are? You have enough clothes; you can work; you can earn money; and you are not crippled. Why are you here? Do you want to laugh at me or make fun of me? You say you will give me everything you have but you have nothing I can use. I need food, clothes, a place to sleep and my health."

"And he (Peter) took him by the right hand and raised him up, and immediately his feet and ankles were made strong." Not only material things in life are vital. In addition, we can hope for the spiritual.

Peter and John were respected men while the cripple was only a tramp wearing shabby clothes and unbathed. Despite the beggar's outward appearance, these men gave him their concern. They gave themselves in the name of Jesus Christ. They only gave him love but this was a special love and much more valuable than the beggar realized. It was God's love which also you and I can possess, and which we can give to others.

When the beggar took Peter's hand, he showed his faith in Peter and accepted his charity. Without his faith and acceptance, the beggar would not have been able to stand.

Frequently today, we are no different from the beggar. Often we have difficulty letting God's love come into our lives, the love and concern which comes from people near us as in our story. Maybe we do not think we deserve help and understanding from our neighbours. Maybe we do not have enough faith to know that others want the best for us. We might ask, "Why do you for care me?" Often we cannot answer this question. "I love you for no other reason, than because you are you, and because you are important to me." We cannot explain our love for someone.

Peter and John valued the beggar only because he was a human being. John Updike dramatizes this in his novel "The Centaur". Peter Caldwell, an 18-year-old boy, has the skin disease psoriasis and is very conscious of it. He thinks people do not like him and do not want to be near him because of his skin condition. He likes Penny very much, in fact he loves her but he is afraid to tell her about his illness for fear she will no longer pay attention to him. Finally, he decides he must tell her. Here is their conversation:

> "'I can't do anything about it, except apologize.'
> 'Aren't you silly', she laughs, 'I knew you had a skin thing. It shows on your face.'
> 'My Gosh, does it, badly?'
> 'No it's not noticeable at all.'
> 'Then you don't mind it?' he asks.
> 'Of course not, you can't help it. It's part of you.'
> 'Is that really how you feel?'
> 'If you knew what love was, you wouldn't ask such a silly question.'"

Penny hits the nail on the head. She makes sure Peter knows her love is much more profound than only skin deep. Penny tells Peter an untruth when she says his skin blemish is not at all noticeable. As far as she is concerned, her love for him is far deeper than this blemish; for her it is not noticeable. She sees his inner being and not only his skin. She loves him for his total self and not merely for his outward appearance.

Similarly, God knows all our problems and difficulties. We cannot hide anything from him. He knows we often see ourselves as unsatisfactory individuals but this does not trouble him. He judges us according to our own abilities and not according to abilities of others. Like Penny, God does not look only at our outer physical and mental stature, instead he judges us on how we use our physical and mental abilities. Therefore, we want to develop and use our God-given talents to our fullest. We all have different abilities, some larger some smaller, but all are important in God's eyes.

Further we all have unused gifts to be developed. The more we use our talents the more we will be able to develop them. When they remain stagnant however they probably will be lost. When looking at the "Parable of the Talents" we find that the third servant was afraid to double his talent. Therefore, since he did not try to increase what he was given, he lost everything. As a result, his master cast him out.

In this novel, Peter Caldwell's father is a teacher. We find Mr. Caldwell telling his students it is more important to develop the talents they have rather than to try to develop talents which they wish they had or talents they thought they should have. He says to Judy, one of his poorer students, "Now Judy, listen to me....everybody has something even if it's just being alive. The good Lord didn't put us here to worry about what we don't have."

Peter Caldwell on the other hand, wants to ignore his mechanical abilities because he admires a certain person who excels in another area. When talking with Peter, Mr. Caldwell says, "Don't bury your talent in the ground. Let your light shine."

Mr. Caldwell suggests that Judy probably has undeveloped talents she could develop. Moreover, Peter could be a good mechanic, if he only applied himself and if he did not think he had to be like someone else whom he admired.

Each of us has to realize we are all individuals; we cannot all fit into the same pattern and be identical to someone else. We cannot live with freethinking traits and have rewarding lives if we copy other people. We only need to be ourselves.

Just as Penny loves and accepts Peter Caldwell the way he is, so God loves us and accepts us as we are. Peter does not have to apologize to Penny for his skin condition and neither do we need to apologize to God for the way we are. We may think we are insufficient because we are not like other people whom we consider superior. We are not inferior; we are different and we have varied intelligences, but not lesser or greater intellects, rather diverse mental powers.

When we know God wants only the best for us, we can give this supreme love to others, as Penny unconditionally loves Peter. Peter finally had faith in Penny's true, unlimited compassion for him. When we know God cares for us as we are, we are able to love and appreciate ourselves. Then our fellow citizens can feel our love and concern we have for them. Only when first loving ourselves can we love those near us.

Peter set aside the selfish thinking about his skin and went beyond the superficial. If we can rise above our self-centeredness and accept the life God has planned for us, we will live happy and rewarding lives. If we are less disturbed about our insufficient selves and more concerned about what we can give others, contentment and meaning will fill our lives. God's unconditional love gives us the power to grow in our lives. With this

Christian development, our lives are changed and we are able to reach out to others giving them the care and understanding they need.

Again, we are reminded of God's love extended to the lame beggar through Peter and John, in the name of Jesus Christ. These two men had no silver or gold so they gave the beggar what they had. The crippled man accepted their love and made no apologies for his condition, thus with his faith and God's power invested in Peter and John he stood and walked.

In a similar manner, Peter Caldwell accepted Penny's love and became well, mentally, emotionally and spiritually. Sometimes we have difficultly knowing God's love and believing it's validity, as did Peter in the first part of his life.

Because Peter and John knew and experienced this divine empathy in Jesus, they were able to receive the crippled beggar as he was and give him their love and concern. This, combined with the faith of the beggar, made the healing possible. Without accepting God's love, healing is impossible.

No longer was the beggar physically or psychologically crippled. He was spiritually healed and now he could offer God's love and care to others around him. We can do the same by letting divine compassion enter into our lives enabling us to provide more life to our fellow citizens.

Even though an individual possesses divine love, he may be unable physically to heal another person, as was possible for Peter and John. Healing depends not only on divine love but also on the spiritual consciousness of the healer. In addition, the one in ill health must be spiritually receptive to his healing.

Love is unlimited in size; it is the most meaningful part of life; yes, it is life itself. Love is not definable in human terms.

In concluding, we read in I. Corinthians 13, 4-8a:

"Love is patient and kind; love is not jealous or boastful; it is not arrogant or rude. Love does not insist on its own way; it is not irritable or resentful; it does not rejoice at wrong, but rejoices in the right. Love bears all things, believes all things, hopes all things, endures all things. Love never ends."

Love is indeed more; it is undefinable in words.

Prayer: Let us pray.

Dear Lord sometimes it is difficult for us to acknowledge and accept your love. Help us to be open to your compassion for us and allow us to let you come into our lives even with the sometimes inferior ideas we have of ourselves. Let us know that your love for us is genuine, freely given, and unconditional. Now as we leave Shin Kwang Church today, let us be able to communicate to others that you also love and care for them. Let them know that you are always in their presence. We ask this in the name of Jesus Christ, the one who taught us love. Amen.

Benediction:

> Our Lord our God, creator of the universe and every living creature within,
> Jesus the Christ and example we are to follow in our daily lives,
> The Holy Spirit our helper in all times of trouble and sorrow,
> and in times of joy and happiness,
> be with every one of us forever and ever and until we meet again. AMEN

Forgiveness

Seong Nam, Shin Kwang Church, Nov. 1, 2008

Sunday School Message

In the Old Testament we read in Proverbs 20: 22: "Don't repay evil with evil. Wait for the Lord to handle the matter."

Forgiveness is something good.

Have you ever said when someone who has done you wrong: "I'm going to get even with him and hurt him too. That will serve him right! He deserves my punishment."

This is a common reaction at first. But sometimes we not only say we will hurt someone; we actually do hurt someone who has hurt us. We can physically hurt someone. Or we can say bad things about someone, which might not even be true. Even if it is true we shouldn't hurt them. I have hurt people with words who have hurt me, but I should have forgiven them and asked God to be with us and help us. Have you ever hurt someone because he has hurt you? *(Children's response)*

God's job is to judge and punish, if it is necessary. We don't honor God when we try to do his job. If we judge or punish other children or adults, God doesn't like that. If we think we can do a better job than God we are mistaken. When we hurt someone we are doing wrong; when we forgive someone we are doing right. This means, we know God will do what is right with that person. We should not judge him. God will judge him. Our job is to forgive him. Maybe if we gave love to other people and forgave them, they would stop doing wrong things.

Again in the Bible, Proverbs says: "Don't repay evil with evil. Wait for the Lord to handle the matter."

Prayer:

Dear Lord, if someone hurts us with his fist or with his mouth, it is hard to forgive that person. Please help us to be able to forgive these people. We want to love our enemies as people, but not love the wrong things they do. Only you can judge these people.

Thank you God for our friends. In Jesus' name, Amen.

성령을 경험하며 다른 선택은 없습니다

(2008 년5 월25 일 성남의 신광 교회에서 그리고 어느 날 두바이 한인 제일 교회에서)

말씀 요나서1 장1 절에서3 장3 절 상반부

성령의 오심 즉 기독교 교회의 시작인 성령강림절을 지난주 우리는 기념했습니다. 그래서 오늘 저는 성령에 관한 저의 세 번째 설교를 하려고 합니다. 제 안에서 성령이 일하심으로 왜 제가 목사가 되어야 하는지를 저로 하여금 깨닫게 하셨습니다. 성령이 저에게 그랬던 것처럼 여러분의 인생을 이끈다는 것을 자각하고 있는 것이 필수적입니다.

사실 저는 목사가 되고 싶지 않았습니다. 진심으로 원하지 않았지만 저에게는 다른 선택이 없었습니다.

대학교에 다니던 여름 방학 때, 알라스카 수렵부를 위해 알라스카 황야에서 일하고 있었습니다. 여전히 제게 큰 흥미를 주었던 매력적인 일이었습니다. 그때에 저는 오로지 생물학자가 되기만을 원했었습니다.

1965 년 여름 저는 제가 살던 앵커리지에서 약 50 마일 (약 80km 혹은 205 리) 가량 북쪽에 위치한 알라스카의 팔머라는 곳에서 일했습니다. 저는 거기서 수렵부 비행기 조종사와 함께 1200 평방 마일이 넘는 지역을 날아다니는 아주 재미있는 일을 했습니다. 조종사와 차를 가지고, 그곳에 사는 큰사슴의 서식지 식물을 조사했습니다. 게다가, 지형도 위의 다양한 관목 종류를 관찰하고 항공 사진을 사용하여 식물군의 다양성을 기술했습니다. 추가적으로, 비행기로, 차로, 혹은 걸어서 대규모의 나뭇잎 표기 기호들을 만들었습니다. 이것은 엄청나게 고무적인 생태학 취업의 기회를 주는 여름이었습니다.

하루는 제 상사 조(Joe)가 "새로 조사해야 할 지역이 있다." 고 말했습니다. 그는 잘 알려진 빅 레이크의 서쪽은 연구할 필요가 없다는 것을 덧붙이며 우리가 어느 곳을 가야 하는지 저에게 지도를 보여주었습니다. 하지만 빅 레이크의 서쪽이 저의 목적이었습니다. 저의 아버지가 어느 정도 소유하고 있는 땅이 있었기에 언젠가 그곳을 발전시키는 것에 흥미가 있었습니다.

그 다음날 저는 조(Joe)가 분명히 그곳에 가지 말라고 했음에도 불구하고 소유하고 있는 크록 호수로 곧장 운전해 갔습니다. 제가 어디로 운전하고 있는지 조차 잊고 저는 이 여행과 그 아름다운 전경을 즐기고 있었습니다. 제가 목적지에 도착했을 무렵 오전 11 시 길이 갑작스럽게 좁아지기 시작했습니다. 그래서 저는 차를 돌릴 장소를 찾아야 했습니다. 되돌아가려고 했을 때, 상황은 더 문제가 되었습니다. 반대 방향으로 가려고 제가 할 수 있는 모든 것을 해 보았지만 제 모든 노력들은 허사였습니다. 거의4 시간 후에도 저는 상황을 나아지게 할 수 없었습니다.

이 작은 길의 왼쪽에는 늪이 있었고, 오른쪽에는 가파른 산마루가 있었습니다. 제가 차를 돌리려고 했을 때 불행하게도 저의 차는, 차 앞의 한 나무와 오른쪽의 한 나무 사이에 끼워졌습니다. 저의 소형 밴은 좁은 길과 수직으로 둑을 반이나 올라 가 있었습니다. 저는 차를 들어 올리고 왼쪽으로 밀었지만, 오히려 더 위태로운 궁지에 몰렸습니다.

이제 저는 절망적이었습니다. "그곳에 가지 마" 라고 하던 죠(Joe)의 말을 기억했습니다. 그때에는 그곳은 거의 인적이 없는 곳이었습니다. 약 10 마일 (16km 혹은 41 리) 떨어진 곳에 다른 좁은 길이 있긴 했지만 누구에게도 거의 사용되지 않았던 길이었습니다. 그 즐거웠던 드라이브도 돈이 드는 것이었지만 만약 제가 차를 거기에 남겨둔다면 그것은 더 많은 돈을 낭비하는 것이었습니다. 그리고는 걷기 시작했습니다. 필마까지 히치하이킹이 가능하다면. 그러나 이 길에는 거의 차가 지나가지 않는데 차를 얻어 타는 것도 거의 희박했습니다. 걷기에 너무 멀었습니다. 내가 무엇을 해야 하지? 하루가 끝날 때 즈음에라도 필마에 도착하면 좋겠는데.. 죠(Joe)가 너무 화내지 않았으면 좋겠다고 생각했습니다. 모든 것이 불가능해 보였습니다.

약 100 피트 (30m) 도 못 가서 저는 멈추고 스스로에게 말했습니다. "여기에 차를 버려둘 순 없어. 절대로."

제가 차로 걸어 돌아가던 그 운명적인 오후, 갑자기 저는 5 살 이었을 때가 생각났습니다. "나는 크면 목사님이 되고 싶어요." 라고 말했습니다. 주일이면 교회에서 설교단 위 높이 서 있는 목사님을 항상 존경했습니다. 5 살인 저에게 그의 깊은 목소리와 폭넓은 위상은 아주 인상적이었습니다. 보통 어린 남자아이들은 경찰관이나 소방관, 군인, 의사 또는 그와 같은 것들이 되고 싶다고 합니다. 그러나 분명히 목사는 아니죠. 오래지 않아 저는 제 꿈을 잊어버렸습니다. 제가 목사가 되어야겠다고 느꼈던 14, 15 살 될 때까지 말입니다. 어쨌든 이런 생각을 저의 어머니 말고는 아무에게도 말하지 않았습니다. 제 친구들이 저를 종교적인 아이라고 생각하기를 원치 않았기 때문이었습니다. 학창시절에는 대학교 가는 것을 준비했고 대학교에서는 생물학을 공부했습니다. 이때에는 진실로 목사가 되고 싶지 않았지만 마음속으로는 신학을 공부해야 한다는 것을 알았습니다. 이것이 저의 운명이었을까요? 시간이 말해주었듯이 저에게는 다른 선택이 없었습니다!

저의 이야기로 돌아가서, 저는 이 길에 저의 소형 밴을 두고 갈 수 없다는 것을 알았습니다. 그래서 저는 제가 혐오하고 경멸하는 일을, 아주 이기적인 일이었지만 인간적인 일이기도 한 일을 했습니다. 바로 요나가 이렇게 했습니다. 그리고 아마도 여기 있는 우리 대부분이 어려운 상황에 있을 때 이렇게 했을 것입니다. 하나님께 혹은 누군가에게 한번쯤 이렇게 말했을 것입니다. "나를 위해 네가 이것을 해주면, 나는 너를 위해 저것을 해 줄게." 요나가 하나님께 고했습니다. "만약 하나님께서 저를 이 물고기의 배에서 꺼내어 주시면 저는 하나님께서 바라시는 것처럼 니느웨에 가서 하나님의 복음을 전하겠습니다." 저는 하나님께 이렇게 고했습니다. "좋습니다. 만약 주님께서 제가 목사가 되기를 원하신다면 그렇게 하겠습니다. 한가지 조건이 있습니다. 저를 여기서 1 시간 안에 꺼내어 주시는 조건 하에서입니다." 저는 하나님과 거래를 했습니다.

저는 계속해서 차를 꺼내려고 시도했습니다. 그러나 차는 앞으로도 이제는 뒤로도 운전할 수 없게 되었습니다. 그렇지만 저는 늪에서 빠져 나오면 방향을 돌릴 수 있을 것 같았습니다. 물론 그리고 나면 어떻게 될지 알았습니다. 솔직히 말해서 무엇을 해야 할지 상상할 수가 없었습니다. 그래서 제가 기대할 수 없었던 어떤 답을 찾으려고 하면서 이 아주 좁은 길을 향해 목적 없이 그저 걸었습니다. 생각 반 기도 반. 25 피트 (8m) 가량 천천히 걸었습니다. 그 때 갑자기 기적이 나타났습니다. 지름 8 인치 (20cm) 가로로 갈라져서 6 피트 (1.8m) 길이의 통나무를 발견했습니다. 이 통나무가 어떻게 거기에 있었는지 정확히 헤아릴 수가 없었습니다. 이 부근에서 유일한 목재였고 제가 필요한대로 정확하게 잘라져 있었습니다. 두 개의 반쪽을 가지고 차의 뒷바퀴 뒤 늪 안으로 목재들을 놓았습니다. 그리고는 짧게 기도했습니다. 제가 널빤지 위로 소형 밴을 늪 안으로 천천히 뒤로 운전했을 때 바퀴들이 널빤지로부터 미끄러지지 않기를 원했습니다. 두 조각 위 뒷바퀴들과 함께 저는 늪의 중간에 있었습니다. 확 움직이지 않도록 기어를 조심조심 앞으로 옮겼습니다. 바퀴가 널빤지들로부터 늪 안으로 미끄러지지 않았습니다. 지금까지는 좋아! 갑자기 무언가가 미끄러지더니 멈춰서 저는 거의 숨을 참았습니다. 만약 나뉘어진 목재들로부터 바퀴가 미끄러졌다면 저한테 플랜 B 는 없었습니다. 그리고는 무사히 단단한 땅으로 다시 한 번 천천히 저는 운전했습니다. 얼마나 행운입니까? 한 시간 후도 아닌 10 분 안으로 저는 운전해 나갈 수 있었습니다. 예, 저는 큰 약속을 했습니다. 확실하게 저의 목표가 아닌 목사가 되겠다고 했습니다. 어떤 무언가가 제가 정확하게 사용할 수 있는 나무를 놓아 놓음으로써 저에게 의사소통을 하려고 했을까요? 우연이었을까요?

그날 오후에 조(Joe)가 야외 작업을 마치고 집으로 돌아가고 있을 때 조(Joe)의 차도 두 개의 타이어가 펑크가 났었습니다. 어떤 사람이 한 개도 아닌 두 개나 타이어 펑크가 나겠습니까? 조(Joe)는 제가 와서 타이어 고치는 것을 도와 주기를 약 6 시까지 기다리고 또 기다렸습니다. 마침내 약 9 시경 제가 도착했을 때 그는 이미 그곳에 없었습니다. 다음 날 제가 어디에 있었는지 그가 물었을 때 저는 거짓을 말하면서 물론, 믿을 수 있는 이야기를 꾸며댔습니다.

다음 주일 저는 앵커리지로 예배를 드리러 갔습니다. 거기에 가서 목사님 (Ralph Week)께 나의 경험을 말씀 드리고 목사가 되고 싶다고 이야기 하려고 했습니다. 예배 후 제가 목사님과 악수를 할 때 그런 사적인 이야기를 많은 사람들이 듣는 곳에서 할 수가 없다고 예배시간 동안 저는 생각했습니다. "목사님께서 만약 점심 초대를 하시면, 내 생각을 말할 수 있을 것 같다" 고 생각했습니다.

예배 후, 저는 목사님과 악수했고 목사님이 말씀했습니다. "있잖아요, 오늘 점심에 초대하고 싶습니다." 저는 진짜 놀랐고 충격을 받았습니다. 성령 하나님께서 두 번째로 저에게 이야기 하시는 걸까요? 아니면 우연의 일치일 뿐일까요? 점심때 저는 또 한번 아무 말도 하지 않았습니다. 왜냐하면 테이블에 사람들이 너무 많아서 그렇게 개인적으로 말할 수 없기 때문이었습니다. 사실 그것은 저의 변명이었습니다.

그 해 여름은 빨리 지나갔고 저는 저의 경험에 대해 더 이상 생각하지 않았습니다. 그 해 여름이 끝날 때쯤 저는 오리건에 있는 조지 폭스 대학으로 돌아갔습니다. 크리스마스 때 저는 앵커리지로 다시 돌아갔습니다. 그리고 이번에는 목사님과 이야기했습니다. 목사님은 신학교 세 곳을 추천해 주셨지만 다시 저는 어떤 한 곳도 지원하지 않았습니다.

오리건으로 돌아 온 어느 날 저녁, 룸메이트가 4 개월 후 졸업 후에 제가 무엇을 할지 물었습니다. 우리 둘 다 6 월이면 졸업을 하는 것이었고 저는 모르겠다고 말했습니다. 저는 진짜 무엇을 해야 할지 몰랐습니다. 실제로 저의 목표였던 야생동물 관리를 전공할 수도 있었지만, 신학을 해야겠다는 생각이 더 강했습니다. 저는 목사가 되기 싫었습니다. 왜냐하면 글을 잘 쓸 자신도 없었고 제 자신이 진짜 크리스천인지도 확실하지 않았기 때문이었습니다. 저는 소위 크리스천들이 가지는 생각과 사상을 가지고 있지 않다고 생각했습니다. 저는 사실이 아닌 것 혹은 제가 믿지도 않는 설교를 하고 싶지 않았습니다.

룸메이트와의 이 대화가 있은 후 저는 방으로 가서 계속 생각했습니다. 저는 제 삶을 어떻게 이끌어야 할지 진짜 알지 못했습니다. 하지만 저는 빨리 결정을 해야한다는 것은 알았습니다. 저는 예수님이 역사 안에서 어떤 일을 하신지 확신하지 못했습니다. 그래서 제가 비록 신기한 성령의 체험을 하긴 했어도 예수님은 단지 좋고 유용한 사람일 뿐이다 라고 말했습니다. 그랬습니다. 그 이상도 아니었습니다. 예수님은 하나님이 아니었습니다. "목사가 되지 않고 생물학자가 될 거야." 저는 드디어 결정을 내렸습니다. 그러면 나의 약속은 어떻게 되는 거지? 제가 이런 결정을 하자마자 한번도 느껴보지 못했던 아주 나쁜 기분이 느껴졌습니다. 제 안에서부터 모든 것이 뜯어져 나오는 것 같이 느껴졌습니다. 그것은 너무 어둡고 공허한 어두움이어서 형용할 수 조차 없었습니다. 저는 지옥을 경험한 적이 없었습니다. 이것은 저에게 지옥의 경험이었고 다시는 이런 경험을 하고 싶지 않습니다. 요나도 또한 물고기 뱃속에서 지옥을 경험했습니다.

그러나 하나님은 큰 물고기로 하여금 요나를 삼키게 하셨습니다. 요나는 3 일 밤낮을 물고기 뱃속에 있으면서 그의 하나님에게 기도했습니다. (그의 기도 후) 하나님은 물고기로부터 요나를 마른 땅에 뱉어내게 했습니다. 두 번째로 성령 하나님께서 요나에게 말씀하셨습니다. "요나야, 큰 성 니느웨로 가서 내가 너에게 가르쳐준 복음을 전하거라." 그래서 요나는 하나님께 순종했고 니느웨로 갔습니다.

요나는 온 힘을 다해 하나님께 용서를 구하며 기도했습니다. 그는 하나님이 그에게 두번째 기회를 준 후 니느웨로 향했습니다. 그는 예언자로서 또한 하나님의 메신저로서 니느웨로 갔습니다. 마침내 요나는 하나님께 순종했습니다.

룸메이트와의 대화가 있은 후 저는 아주 혼란스러웠고 예수님이 어떤 의미인지 알 수 없었습니다. 제 안에 있었던 그 어두움과 공허는 너무 끔찍해서 저의 확신을 바꾸지 않고는 인생을 살아갈 수가 없었습니다. 이 경험은 저에게 큰 인상을 남겼고 예수님이 단지 좋고 유용한 분 이상이라는 것을 알았습니다. 비록 제 감정과 경험을 다 이해할 수는 없었지만 예수님이 구주이고 하나님이라는 것을 인정할 수 있었습니다. 그리고 저는 침대 곁에 무릎을 꿇고 용서될 수 없는 저의 죄를 하나님께서 용서해 주시기를, 그리고 하나님께서 이 끔찍한 기분을 떨칠 수 있도록 해 주시기를, 제가 할 수 있는 한 간절하게 기도했습니다. 제 생애 그렇게 열심히 기도해 본 적이 없었습니다. 저는 목사가 되겠다고 한번 더 약속했습니다. 성령 하나님께서는 저에게 세 번 이야기 하셨습니다. 그리고 이번에 저는 그분께 순종했습니다.

모든 크리스천들이 다른 믿음, 신념, 다양한 종교적인 이해를 가지고 있다는 것을 저는 압니다. 이것은 반드시 그렇습니다. 모든 사람들이 다양한 인격, 배경, 교육, 그리고 다른 종류의 지능을 가지고 있기 때문입니다. 이 모든 크리스천의 다양함 때문에, 우리는 서로에게서 배우고 동시에 같은 교회에서 예배를 드립니다.

그 다음 날 저는 3 통의 편지를 세 신학교에 보냈습니다. 그리고 그 해 여름이 끝날 무렵 몇 통의 편지가 왔다 갔다 한 후, 샌프란시스코 신학교에서 한 통의 전화를 받았습니다. 다음주 월요일 바로 공부할 수 있다고 했습니다. 벌써 금요일이었고 월요일 아침 저는 캘리포니아 샌 안셀모에 있는 샌프란시스코 신학교로 날아가서 신학을 공부하기 시작 했습니다.

성도 여러분, 이것은 제 개인적 이야기입니다. 우리 각자는 다 간증거리가 있고 그것은 다 다릅니다. 그리고 그런 경험을 하는 것이 꼭 필요한 것만은 아닙니다. 성령 하나님께서는 다른 방법으로 우리 모두에게 이야기 하시며, 대부분 우리가 그의 목소리를 듣기 기대할 때 이야기 하시는 것은 아닙니다. 어떠하든지 우리가 성령 하나님께서 우리에게 말하실 때 그의 음성을 듣는 것이 중요합니다. 그리고 나서 우리는 그에게 긍정적인 답을 해야 합니다. 이것은 종종 힘과 용기가 많이 필요합니다. 그러나 하나님의 도우심으로, 성령 하나님의 힘으로 모든 것이 가능합니다. 우리가 하나님의 도움을 구할 때 성령님께서 우리를 도우실 것입니다!

오늘 저는 아주 행복합니다. 제가 마침내 성령 하나님께서 말씀하시는 것을 들었을 뿐만 아니라 더 나아가 긍정적으로 대답했기 때문입니다. 저는 "네, 하나님, 목사가 되겠습니다." 라고 했습니다. 그리고 저는 약속을 지켰습니다. 저에게는 목사가 되는 것 외에 다른 선택은 없었습니다. 저는 제가 성령 하나님께 순종하지 않았다면 제 삶이 얼마나 공허했을지 압니다.

기도:

하나님, 우리가 하나님의 음성을 잘 받아들일 수 있도록 도와주십시오. 하나님께서 우리에게 말씀하실 때 들을 수 있을 뿐 아니라 하나님께서 원하시는 삶을 살아가도록 도와주십시오. 말씀에 긍정적으로 대답하고 하나님의 이끄심을 따라가길 원합니다. 우리의 의지가 아닌 하나님의 뜻대로 우리가 할 수 있도록 인도해 주십시오. 예수님 이름으로 기도합니다. 아멘

축도:

우주와 그 안의 모든 살아 있는 것들의 주재이신 우리의 하나님께서

우리의 날마다의 삶에서 따르기로 한 예수 그리스도께서

문제와 슬픔이 있을 때나 기쁨과 행복이 있을 때나 우리의 조력자이신 성령님께서

모든 우리 하나하나에게 지금부터 영원까지 있으리로다. 아멘

번역: 구경옥(translated by Kyung Ok Koo)

죽는다는 것은 산다는 것

말씀: 요한복음 11 장 17-44 절

저와 나이가 같거나 저보다 젊은데 죽은 친구들이나 친척들에 관해 제가 신문에서 읽거나 들었을 때, 이 세상에서 얼마나 더 오래 살까 제 자신에게 묻습니다. 미래에 저를 위해 무엇이 더 있을까요? 제가 잘 살까요 아니면 고로운 삶을 살까요? 영생에 대해 알지 못하기 때문에 죽는 것을 두려워하는 사람들과 목사로서 이야기 했었습니다. 몇몇은 이생이 끝났을 때 더 이상 기대할 것이 없다고, 그래서 그들에게는 어떤 종류의 미래에 대한 진실도 없다고 믿었습니다.

여기서 말씀은 나흘 전 나사로가 죽은 베다니로 예수님께서 들어가시는 것을 묘사하고 있습니다. 히브루 전통에 따르면, 육체가 혼과 다시 결합하여 다시 살아있는 사람이 되리라는 희망으로 사람이 죽은 후 삼 일을 영혼이 육체 가까이에서 계속 맴돈다고 합니다. 그러나, 삼일 후, 육체가 썩기 시작하면 영혼은 떠난다고 합니다. 나사로의 경우, 육체가 부패되기 시작하면, 육체가 혼과 재결합하기에 불가능하다고 히브루 사람들이 믿었기 때문에, 사일 째가 중요했습니다. 예수님께서 나사로를 사일 째에 육체적으로 살리셨기 때문에 기적은 훨씬 더 위대했습니다.

그러나 오늘날 우리는 육체의 부활보다는 영적인 부활에 관심을 가집니다. 예수님 역시 영적 되살림을 의미하셨습니다. 마리아와 마르다는 육체의 부활을 원했고 기대했습니다. 예수님께서 겨우 2 마일 (약 3.2km 혹은 8 리) 떨어진 예루살렘에 계시면서 사일 째가 될 때까지 여전히 나사로의 죽음을 보러 오시지 않았기 때문에 그들은 예수님에게 화가 나 있었습니다. 지금 육체의 부활은 가능하지 않을 것이라고 생각했습니다. 예수님께서는 마르다에게 말씀하셨습니다. "너의 형제는 다시 살아날 것이다." 그녀는 예수님을 믿었고, 말했습니다. "마지막 날, 심판의 날에 그가 다시 살아날 것이라는 것을 알고 있어요." 독실한 바리새인들과 다른 이스라엘 사람들에게 이 믿음은 아주 흔한 것이었습니다. 예수님께서는 그들의 믿음 때문에 바리새인들을 비판하시거나 쫓아내지 않으셨습니다. 그러나, 예수님께서는 그들의 현재와 영적인 삶이 어디에서부터 왔는지를 마르다와 모든 다른 사람들이 알기를 원하셨습니다. 이때에는 예수님께서 심판 날의 삶을 염려하지 않으셨습니다. 예수님께서 말씀하셨습니다. "나는 부활이요 생명이니 누구든지 나를 믿는 자는 (육체적으로) 죽어도 (영적으로) 살겠고, 살아서 나를 믿는 자는 영원히 죽지 않으리라. " 이 말씀은 예수님을 무조건 믿으면 영생을 가지리라는 뜻입니다. 마지막 날의 부활만이 중요한 것은 아닙니다. 오늘날의 영적인 부활도 똑같이 매우 중요합니다. 이것이 우리가 알고 경험할 수 있는 알려지지 않은 신비로운, 영적인 오늘날의 거듭남입니다. 물론 마르다는 매우 슬펐습니다. 그녀의 형제를 잃었습니다. 논의가 어떻게 계속되는가를 우리가 살펴볼 때, 우리의 궁금증은 커 갑니다. 마르다는 평화로웠고 감정을 조절하고 있었습니다. 그녀의 확고한 정신적 힘, 믿음, 신념을 설명하기가 쉽지 않습니다. 예수님께서 육체의 부활을 위해 삼일 안에 오실 것이라는 깊은 희망을 그녀가 가졌었다 라고 우리는 이해할 수 있습니다. 예수님, 나사로, 마리아, 마르다가 몇 년에 걸친 아주 가까운 관계였기 때문에, 마르다에게 이것은 특별한 실망이었습니다. 상식적으로, 그들은 예수님께서 오셨을 것이라고 믿었습니다. 사일 째까지 예수님께서 도착하지 않으셨을 때, 그녀의 목소리에 왜 못마땅함이 있었는지를 우리는 압니다. "예수님께서 여기 계셨더라면, 저의 형제는 죽지 않았을 거예요. 그러나 저는 지금이라도 예수님께서 하나님께 부탁하는 무엇이나 하나님께서 들어주실 것이라고 알아요." 그녀는 아마도 그녀가 말하는 것이 무엇인지 정확히 알지 못했습니다. 그러나, 그녀는 하나님이 원하시는 무엇이나 하실 수 있을 거라고 알고 있었습니다.

이 세상에서의 삶이 즐겁고 가치 있는 것일지라도, 우리가 이 세상을 떠날 때까지 우리의 삶 속에서 최후의 것을 찾을 수 없습니다. 하나님께로부터 오는 모든 것을 우리가 이해하지 못하지만, 우리가 하나님께 신념을 구하고 하나님을 믿으면 하나님을 증거할 수 있는 하나님의 뜻과 용기에 따라 사는 힘을 주신다는 것을 우리는 알고 있습니다. 그때 우리는 성취와 평화를 찾게 됩니다.

항상 죽음은 우리들이 이해하기 어렵습니다. 언제 혹은 왜 사람이 그의 육체를 반드시 떠나야만 하는지를 알지 못합니다. 삶과 죽음 둘 다 알려지지 않은 이유로, 알려지지 않은 근원으로부터 옵니다. 생물학, 화학, 물리학으로 우리가 존재하는 근원을 설명할 수 있을지도 모릅니다. 그러나 우리의 현실의 목적은 많은 이들에게 불명확하게 남아 있습니다. 이 알려지지 않은 힘을 저는 "하나님" 이라고 하겠습니다. 우리가 아는 모든 것은, 탄생은 반드시 죽음을 동반한다는 것입니다.

그러나 친애하는 성도 여러분, 육체의 죽음은 새로운 삶, 곧 너무도 강력하면서 상상할 수도 없는 영적 삶을 가져다 줍니다. 비록 이 새 삶이 우리에게 알려져 있지 않다 하더라도, 오늘의 말씀과 다른 성경 구절을 통해 모든 믿는 자들이 이 세상에서 시작할 수 있는 영원한 삶을 쌓아 왔다는 것을 우리는 압니다. 낯선 사람들, 난민들, 우리가 모르는 혹은 감사하지도 않는 다른 사람들을 포함하여 모든 사람들을 향해 우리가 사랑과 연민을 가지고 있을 때, 행복과 평화와 조화는 기독교의 상급이 됩니다.

기쁨과 사랑이 우리로부터 발산될 때, 이 새롭고 쌓아온 영원한 삶이 우리 안에 있습니다. 사랑은 우리의 얼굴로부터 발하여 흘러갑니다. 우리를 둘러싼 모두에게 친절과 이해를 보여주면서 지금 우리는 살고 있습니다. 새 삶을 누리면서 그것들로부터 훨씬 더 많은 에너지를 느낄 수 있습니다.

제가 11 살 즈음 저의 할머니께서 돌아가시기 직전에 그녀는 지혜롭게 말했습니다. "나는 죽을 준비가 되었구나." 계속 말씀하시기를 "내가 모든 것을 생각해 볼 때, 나는 죽는 것이 행복하구나." 라고 하셨습니다. 11 살 아이로서 제가 무엇을 생각했을지 여러분은 상상할 수 있습니까? 어떻게 사람이 죽기를 원할 수 있지? 저는 무슨 말을 할 수 있었을까요? 사람이 혼이 되었을 때 훨씬 더 나은 현실이 있다고 할머니께서 말씀하셨습니다. 그것은 완전히 다른 삶 입니다. 묘사할 수도 이해할 수도 없고, 심지어는 정확하게 생각할 수도 없는 것입니다. 오직 죽음 이후에, 영원한 삶의 두 번째 부분을 우리는 경험할 수 있습니다.

죽음이 우리에게 다다를 때, 그것을 받아들일 신념이 우리에게 있습니까? 어떤 사람들에게 이러한 성경 구절들이 믿기 쉽지 않을지라도, 우리가 하나님의 인도와 보호를 구할 때, 하나님께서 우리가 믿을 수 있도록 도와 주실 것입니다. 1971 년 샌프란시스코의 퍼시픽 의료 센터에서 목사였을 때 제가 만난 17 살 소년을 기억합니다. 그는 지체 부자유자였으며 미소년 같은 요즘의 히피였습니다. 저는 그를 종종 방문했습니다. 우리의 대화 중에, 그는 "내가 죽는다면, 내 신체에서 자유로워져 걷거나 쉽게 움직였을 텐데" 라고 말했습니다. 그때 그는 진심이었습니다. 걷거나 그의 신체 다른 부분들을 쉽게 움직일 수 없었습니다.

이 삶 후에 무언가가 더 있다는 것을 그로 하여금 알게 하는 그의 이해와 믿음이 충분히 강했다라고 한편으로 저는 믿고 있습니다. 불사의 존재로서 어떤 것이 올지 조금은 알고 있었는지도 모릅니다.

더 이상 살아있지 않지만, 저의 할머니와 이 젊은 청년은 지금 영원하고도 영적인 삶을 살고 있다고 저는 믿습니다. 여러분과 제가 이생에서의 육체를 떠날 때 우리가 영적인 형태일 것이라고 또한 확신합니다. 예수님께서 말씀하십니다. "나는 부활이요, (영원한) 생명이요. 나를 믿는 자, 죽어도 살 것이며, 누구든지 살아서 나를 믿는 자는 영원히 살 것이다." 성도 여러분, 죽는 것이 사는 것 입니다. 아멘

축도:

우리가 다시 만날 때까지

여호와는 네게 복을 주시고 너를 지키시기를 원하며

여호와는 그의 얼굴을 네게 비추사 은혜 베푸시기를 원하며

여호와는 그 얼굴을 네게로 향하여 드사 평강 주시기를 원하노라.

예수님의 이름으로 기도합니다. 아멘　　　　번역: 구경옥(translated by Kyung Ok Koo)

Mein Koreanisches Abenteuer

(Kurze Fassung)

Ich erzähle ein paar Höhepunkte und Ereignisse, die ich von 1997 bis 2016 überall in Südkorea erleben durfte. Meine ganze Zeit war immer voll von unglaublichen Eindrücken und wertvollen Erfahrungen. Diese ausserordentliche Geschichte fing an im Oktober 1997 als ich für ein dreiwöchiges Austauschprogramm nach Süd-Korea ausgewählt war. Ein Teil meiner Zeit verbrachte ich auf einem Medizinischen Missionsschiff, das sich um die Inselgruppe in Südwest S. Korea bewegte. Die Mission wurde von der Presbyterianischen Kirche in Korea (PCK) betrieben.

Zur Schiffsbesatzung gehörten der Kapitän, zwei Matrosen, sowie der Schiffsingenieur. Dazu kamen ein Schulmediziner, ein in traditioneller asiatischer Medizin ausgebildeter Arzt, ein Zahnarzt, zwei Krankenschwestern und ein Pfarrer. Das Missionsschiff „Salvation" zog jedes Jahr von März bis Nov. durch das koreanische Süd-Meer und das Gelbe Meer. Jeden Tag legte es bei einer neuen Insel an, um die Leute zu besuchen und medizinisch zu betreuen. Das Evangelium wurde gleichzeitig an die Bewohner dieser über 100 Inseln jährlich missioniert.

Auf dem Schiff sah der Tag so aus: Um 4.30 Uhr wurde meistens eine Andacht gehalten. Um 6.00 Uhr wurden die Generatoren eingeschaltet. Um 6.30 Uhr standen alle auf, die noch im Bett waren, und um 7.00 Uhr wurde gegessen. Um 8.00 Uhr wurde es Zeit für die Morgenmeditation, und sofort anschliessend wurden die Anker gelichtet, und wir fuhren zur nächsten Insel.

Nach unserer Ankunft suchten wir einen geeigneten Ort, um unsere Tagesarbeit auszuführen, entweder in einem Gemeindesaal, Kirchenschiff, oder sonst einem passenden Ort, wo wir Verschiedenes aufstellen konnten, um unsere medizinischen und weiteren Aufgaben zu erfüllen.

An einem Tag benützten wir einen grossen alten Saal, der wahrscheinlich nicht oft gebraucht wurde. Es kamen jetzt ca. 50 alt aussehende Frauen und wenige Männer, die meistens tag-täglich dem kalten Meerwasser und der oft unfreundlichen Witterung ausgesetzt waren. Sie bereiteten Meeresalgennetze vor und setzten sie im Meer aus. Diese Patienten litten häufig an Rheuma, Erkältungen oder Lungenkrankheiten. So wurden oft die gleichen Medikamente und Heilungsmethoden verschrieben. Manchmal hatten sie nicht haargenau die richtigen Medikamente, so mussten sie brauchen was sie hatten. Medikamente wurden oft verschenkt, die hin und wieder abgelaufen waren. Deshalb war wichtig, dass sie immer wieder neue finanzielle Unterstützung bekamen.

In dieser Umgebung ging es nicht nur um die Missionierung und Heilung per se, sondern auch, weil aus gemeinschaftlichen und wirtschaftlichen Gründen diese isolierten Orte gesund bleiben mussten, um Produkte herzustellen, und wenn genügend erzeugt werden konnte, zu exportieren.

Während dem Tag wurde meistens im Saal eine Predigt gehalten, eventuell ein Vortrag über Bluthochdruck, asiatische Naturheilmedizin, oder etwas Ähnliches. Solches richtete sich nach Ort, Zahl der Patienten und unserer verfügbaren Zeit. In einer Ecke, nach der Predigt, meldeten alle sich an für ihren Arztbesuch bei der Krankenschwester. Sie erklärte ihnen u. a., was für Behandlungen sie zu erwarten hatten.

Nach der ärztlichen Untersuchung gingen sie zur Apothekerecke und erhielten dort ihre Medikamente. Wenn verschrieben, was meistens der Fall war, besuchten sie als nächsten Ort den Akupunkteur. Er verrichtete verschiedenartige Akupunkturen, sowie andere asiatische Naturheilmethoden. Oft wurden die Frauen und Männer mit trockenen Wärmepflastern auf dem Rücken 20 bis 30 Min., und/oder mit einem elektrischen Vibrator behandelt. Manchmal wurde auch elektrische Akupunktur verwendet.

An diesem Tag wurde ein grosser Vorhang aufgehängt, als Schlupfwinkel für alle, die eine Spritze, oder andere persönliche Untersuchung oder Behandlung brauchten. Doch es wurde überall im Raum gespritzt und untersucht, nur nicht hinter dem Vorhang!

Meine Aufgabe war, obwohl ich u. a. in der Apotheke Vorbereitungen getroffen habe, in einer weiteren Ecke für die Patienten am Schluss ihrer Behandlungen mit Handauflegung zu beten. Eine der Krankenschwestern nannte mir nun den Patientennamen, und ob er oder sie Christ sei oder nicht, und woran sie litten. Je nach dieser Information betete ich. Englisch hatten die Patienten meistens nicht verstanden, aber sie berichteten, dass es etwas Besonderes und für sie wichtig war.

Das Mittagessen nahmen wir jetzt alle zusammen im Pfarrerhaus ein, an diesem Tag von Kirchenmitarbeiterinnen vorbereitet. Wir assen am Boden mit gekreuzten Beinen, natürlich Reis, heute, wie oft, mit Fischsuppe. Die Suppe bestand aus Seeschnecken, Meeresalgen, verschiedenen anderen Seepflanzen und -tieren, und Fische mit vielen Gräten; ich sage, „Knochen-Suppe"! Auch hatte es, wie immer, etwa 10 bis 12 kleine Teller mit Gemüse, Fisch, wenig Fleisch, usw. gegeben, alles sehr scharf gewürzt.

Doch, natürlich gibt es auch Fleischgerichte. Die eine sehr bekannte Schweinefleisch-Mahlzeit heisst „Bullgogi", und wird ähnlich wie ein Tischgrill gekocht. „Gegogi" oder höflicher „Poschinta" (Hunde-Fleisch!) wird selten gegessen. Einmal sah ich sogar Katzen auf dem Markt. Dazu ist bei jedem Mahl ihr Nationalgericht „Kimch'i" dabei, aus Sellerie, Kohl, Rüben, Gurken usw. gefertigt. Es ist scharf gewürzt, etwas vergoren; es gibt viele Rezepte, oft geheim von Familien-Frauen zubereitet.

Manchmal befindet sich auf der Speisekarte ein Nudelgericht, aber mit Metall-Stäbchen, die die Koreaner immer brauchen, ist alles sehr rutschig!

Zum Dessert auf der Karte steht z.B., Asiatische Birne, die für uns ungewohnt sind. Das sind grosse, runde, gelb-weisse Früchte, meistens grösser als ein Apfel, aber weniger süss, auf Koreanisch „Bee". Süssigkeiten kennen sie wenig. Sie haben selbstverständlich auch andere Früchte, die wir kennen: Apfel, Banane, Wassermelone, Mandarine, Dattel, Pflaumen, Kaki, Erdbeeren usw. Früchte sind teuer für ihre Verhältnisse, aber werden oft nach dem scharfen Essen als Leckerbissen genossen. Man findet wenig Unterschied zwischen dem Essen am Morgen, Mittag und Abend. Reis und „kimch'i" sind immer dabei. Koreaner sagen, ohne Reis und „kimch'i" tag-täglich zu essen, könnten sie nicht leben.

Normalerweise, nach einem Mittagessen, gingen wir zurück zu der wartenden Menge. Aber, wenn wenige Leute kamen, wurde mit einem Lautsprecher vom Kirchendach aus geworben.

An einem Abend arbeiteten wir länger als normal, deshalb konnten wir mit dem Beiboot, nicht mehr im Tageslicht von der Insel zur „Salvation" zurückfahren. Es wäre zu gefährlich für die Meeresalgenleinen, die dicht im Meer ausgestreut waren. Wir wollten die Ernte nicht zerstören. Es blieb nichts übrig, als dass wir Männer im Saal nebeneinander in einer Reihe schliefen, nachdem wir alles von der medizinischen Tagesbetreuung usw. aufräumten und ein paar Tücher auf dem Boden ausbreiteten. Die Frauen waren auf dem Boden im Pfarrhaus untergebracht. Aber meistens wird sowieso am Boden geschlafen. Bodenheizung, die von Koreanern vor einigen Hundert Jahren entwickelt wurde, ist doch bei ihnen normal, aber kann freilich ein Problem verursachen. Schokolade als Mitbringsel darf am Boden im Gepäck nicht liegen gelassen werden. Schokoladen im Koffer schmelzen, habe ich erlebt — was für eine Schweinerei!

An meinem ersten Abend in Süd-Korea kam Choi Young-Ung „Moksanim" zu mir. „Moksanim" heisst „Herr Pfarrer" auf Koreanisch. Er sagte mir, dass ich am Sonntag eine Predigt zu halten hätte. Das war doch kein Problem, denn eine Predigt hatte ich bereit. Aber meine deutsche Fassung wollte er auf seinem Tisch früh am nächsten Morgen auf Englisch übersetzt haben! Ich wollte sie Englisch vortragen, von meinem deutschen Text, aber für die Übersetzerin genügte das nicht. Damit ich die Übersetzung realisieren konnte, fragte ich nach einem Computer, aber als ich, nach dem Abendessen, im Büro am Computer sass, merkte ich sofort, dass alle Tasten und auch sonst alles auf Koreanisch eingerichtet waren! Choi „Moksanim" stellte alles schnell auf Englisch ein, und verschwand. Jetzt konnte ich arbeiten, aber als ich offenbar eine falsche Taste drückte, war alles wieder auf Koreanisch, und nun was? Ja, ich drückte einige Minuten weitere Tasten, und nichts ist geschehen. Was mache ich jetzt – niemand im Büro – alle zuhause oder im Ausgang?! Plötzlich, Gott sei Dank, war wieder alles auf Englisch! Leider ist dies einige Male passiert, aber um halb eins, 4 Std. später, war ich endlich fertig, „fix und fertig", und müde!

Anekdoten:

Nun erzähle ich kurze Anekdoten, Erlebnisse, Fakten und Lustiges.

– – Auf einmal musste ich an einem Sonntag zwei verschiedene Predigten halten! Am nächsten, Tag bei der Auswertung, fragte ich welche Predigt die Gottesdienstbesucher lieber hörten. Die erste Predigt am Morgen war etwas konservativ und gefühlsbetont; die zweite am Abend eher modern, und für sie etwas progressiv, mit dem Kernpunkt „Frauen und Männer sind gleichwertig und -wichtig". Zu diesem Thema habe ich gesprochen, weil Frauen in Korea vielfach unterdrückt sind. Die älteren Leute interessierten sich eher für die erste Predigt, und die unter 40 eher für die zweite, aber mit Ausnahmen auf beiden Seiten.

– – Einmal, musste ich eine Seniorenveranstaltung frühzeitig verlassen. Mein Übersetzer erklärte mir, ich hätte jetzt eine Rede oder Predigt zu halten; die Uni-Studenten warteten bereits. „Das macht nichts", dachte ich. Eine Rede, oder Predigt, hatte ich immer bei mir. Stets vorbereitet zu sein habe ich gelernt!

– – Auf einmal nach einer Abendandacht, um 23 Uhr, wurde mir die Aufgabe gegeben, um 7 Uhr am nächsten Morgen eine 30-minütige Meditation zu halten! Zwischen meinen Träumen habe ich alles vorbereitet! In Korea habe ich wirklich in Gott vertrauen gelernt.

– – An einem Tag hörten wir etwas früher auf, gingen auf das Schiff zurück, assen hastig, und um 18.20 Uhr sagte der Pfarrer mir, dass ich die Mittwoch-Abend Predigt zu halten hätte, und zwar auf der Insel um 19 Uhr! Das ist alles rasant gegangen, aber so ist das in Korea. Man muss immer bereit sein — für alles! Doch man lernt schnell. Jedenfalls, machte ich mich, so schnell wie möglich, einigermassen bereit. Und um 18.59 Uhr, fand ich mich in der Kirche ein, nach einer 7 Minutenfahrt mit dem Beiboot und einem 4 Minutenlauf vom Boot zur Kirche. Etwas verschwitzt war ich bereit, den Gottesdienst zu halten. Nach dem Gottesdienst teilte ich Schweizerschokolade aus, und die Gottesdienstbesucher waren überglücklich.

– – Manchmal, besonders in meinen ersten Jahren, haben diese Inselbewohner noch nie Europäer gesehen. So wurde hin und wieder, nach einem Gottesdienst oder einer Ansprache, ein Autogramm verlangt, wie an diesem Abend! „Und ich bin doch kein Pop Star", dachte ich!

– – Wieder im Schiff, sammelten wir uns um 22 Uhr im Kreis am Boden, und beteten für die kranken Tagespatienten, alle laut zusammen, und alles durcheinander. Wir erhielten alle unseren eigenen, natürlich Koreanischen Personenbericht, über einen bestimmten Kranken. Koreanisch lesen kann ich kaum, aber beten ist ein Teil meines Berufes!

– – Das Alle-miteinander-beten beunruhigte mich etwas, deshalb veranlasste ich am nächsten Morgen, am Schluss meiner Meditation, dass wir alle in der Stille beten! Das kannten sie wenig.

– – Einmal waren wir zum „Zvieri“ eingeladen. Plötzlich sollte ich im Zimmer nebenan duschen gehen. Eigentlich wollte ich nicht, denn ich war verlegen, bin aber doch gegangen! Man darf nicht nein sagen, weil sie sonst ihr Gesicht verlieren könnten. Es war ein heisser Tag, und ich war wieder etwas verschwitzt. Vielleicht habe ich nicht besonders gut gerochen! Doch alle haben, eine und einer nach dem anderen, geduscht, — ausserhalb der Badewanne! Ja, einen Abfluss hatte es im Fussboden! Nachher, wenn man sauber ist, Zeit hat und möchte, geht man in die Wanne und entspannt sich im warmen Wasser. Das Wannenwasser wird oft mehrmals gebraucht! Ich durfte als erster duschen, aber gebadet habe ich nicht. Auf dem Schiff konnte man meistens nicht duschen, wegen der Wasser-Knappheit.

– – Auf einmal im Bus nahm eine Frau, unerwartet, die Mappe meinem Kollegen aus der Hand ohne Worte, und legte sie auf ihren Schoss. „Was macht sie? Stehlen ist verboten!“ dachte ich. Das ist aber typisch in Korea, wenn jemand mit Gepäck steht, und der andere sitzt. Worte werden nicht gewechselt, und Augenkontakt ist auch unwahrscheinlich. Wenn der eine aussteigen will, gibt ihm der andere sein Gepäck zurück.

– – Einmal beobachtete ich, wie eine Frau die Autotür für einen Mann öffnete, und höflich, nach dem Einsteigen des Mannes, schloss! Auch das ist typisch.

– – Oder einmal erlebte ich, wie eine ältere Dame im Tram aufgestanden ist und mir ihren Platz anbot. Die Frau war sicher 15 Jahre älter als ich. Auch hier musste ich mich anpassen, denn alle Koreaner haben mich angeschaut, als ob ich etwas angestellt hätte. Schliesslich habe ich ihren Platz eingenommen und alles war wieder ruhig. Frauen in Korea haben eindeutig einen tieferen Rang in dieser Männergesellschaft. Doch Frauen verwalten meistens das Geld!

– – Nach dem Haarschneiden werden oft andere Dienstleistungen angeboten, und nicht Maniküre oder Pediküre. Nach meinem Schnitt, in diesem Fall, passte ich mich nicht an, und trat nicht ins hintere Zimmer!

– – Koreaner haben eine andere Beziehung zur „Zeit“. Einmal sollte ich in einem Zimmer 15 Min. warten. Die 15 Minuten dauerten 1 1/2 Std. Jawohl, Lesestoff hatte ich bei mir!

– – Einmal sollte ich um 8.30 Uhr abgeholt werden. Doch um 7 Uhr früh hat es geklingelt. –Ich war gerade in die Dusche gestiegen. Jetzt mussten sie warten! Das passiert immer wieder bei allen! Ein oder zwei Mal sogar erschienen sie, bei mir, überhaupt nicht! Vielleicht sind solche Zeitunterschiede manchmal sprachliche Missverständnissen.

– – Den ersten Geburtstag feiert man wenn man geboren wird. Beim Jahreswechsel wird man zwei Jahre alt. D.h. wenn man am 31. Dez. geboren ist, ist man schon ein Jahr alt, am nächsten Tag, am 1. Jan. ist das eintägige Baby bereits zwei Jahre alt! Wenn man am 1. Jan. geboren ist, muss man ein Jahr warten bis man zwei Jahre alt ist! Also, ein Koreaner ist ein bis zwei Jahre älter als er tatsächlich ist, nach unserer Rechnung.

– – In Korea wechselt der Geburtstag jedes Jahr, denn sie brauchen meistens den Lunar Kalender.

– – Nach einer Predigt, oder einem Gebet, wird häufig geklatscht. Was bedeutet das? Nach meiner Predigt möchte ich, dass die Predigtgänger meditieren statt jubeln.

– – Am Esstisch werden die Knochen von Fisch-Suppe, und alles was man sonst nicht kauen oder essen kann, auf den Tisch ausgespuckt!, — „wie ordinär“, dachte ich. Doch hier habe ich mich angepasst, denn alle taten es, auch die Damen.

– – Wichtige Leute in Korea, oder Leute, die wichtig sein wollen, brauchen einen Lautsprecher! Einmal sassen sich an einem kleinen Tisch ein Prediger und zwei Zuhörer gegenüber. Der Prediger benützte ein Mikrophon für seinen Vortrag. Seine Stimme konnte man überall in der leeren, grossen Kirche hören, — unerhört!

– – Einmal in einer winzigen Kirche sang eine Solistin mit einem Mikrophon so laut, dass ausserhalb der Kirche ihre Stimme weit weg gehört werden konnte. Vielleicht war das Kirchen-Werbung! Doch, ich musste meine Finger in die Ohren stecken, was wenig diente! Alle haben mich beäugt!

– – Beim Schwimmen in Korea legen Frauen ihren Badeanzug an, keine Bikini, und darüber ihre Strassenkleider. Jetzt springen sie ins Wasser!

– – Meistens tragen Männer T-Shirts beim Baden, aber ich nicht, obwohl man mir doch das sehr empfahl! Es war bewölkt, so warum ein T-Shirt? Als ich aus dem Wasser stieg, haben alle mich gemustert, als ob ich eine Sünde begangen hätte! Das nächste Mal trug auch ich ein T-Shirt!

– – Kurz nach meiner Einreise in Korea spazierten wir die Strasse entlang. Sun-jin fragte mich, was ich aus dem Aquarium essen wollte. Als Witz habe ich sofort geantwortet, den Tintenfisch dort! Fünf Minuten später sassen wir am Restauranttisch und assen das halb lebendige Tier. Einmal im Mund wickelten sich die Tentakel um die Zunge herum und klebten im Mund innen. Ich wusste, ich musste ihn schnell verzehren, sonst ersticke ich. Aus diesem Grund dürfen kleine Kinder sie nicht essen.

– – Nase schnäuzen darf man am Tisch nicht. So wird die ganze Zeit geschnüffelt, was ich unangenehm finde.

– – Beim Komplimente machen muss man in Korea immer vorsichtig sein. Bei meinem letzten Besuch 2016 habe ich meine Frau zum ersten Mal in dieses Land der kulturellen Unterschiede mitgenommen. Wir wurden zu einem schönen Abendessen ins „Grand Ambassador Hotel" in Seoul eingeladen. Mary sagte zu Hyang Rae, die auf der anderen Tischseite sass, dass sie eine wunderschöne Brosche trug und sie bewunderte sie. Sofort nahm sie das Schmuckstuck ab und befestigte es an Mary. Mary versuchte so schnell wie möglich die Brosche zurück zu geben, denn sie meinte Hyang Rae sollte den Schmuck nicht verschenken. Doch Hyang Rae und die anderen Koreaner am Tisch meinten Mary müsste es annehmen. Nach einer kurzen Debatte, die Mary verlor, nahm sie das ehrenvolle Prachtstück an, das mit einer natürlichen Perle in der Mitte von rosaroten Korallen umgeben war. Sie trägt es gern, ist nun aber nicht sicher wie sie Komplimente machen sollte! Einige Mal ist mir dieser Koreanische Brauch aufgefallen.

– – Interessant ist: Überall wird WC Papier benützt. Als ich das Papier vom Esstisch entfernen wollte, („Sicher ist ein Fehler gemacht worden", dachte ich.) haben alle am Tisch gesagt, "Nein, nein, das brauchen wir!" WC Papier wird als Servietten und sonst überall gebraucht, auch bei den Ärzten; andere Länder, andere Sitten!

– – Das koreanische Volk ist arbeitsam, grosszügig, und freundlich, aber wenn man sie nicht kennt, können sie manchmal, für uns, arrogant, unhöflich und sogar egoistisch erscheinen.

– – Die Hierarchie in ihrem Leben spielt eine grosse Rolle, deshalb ist eine Visitenkarte mit allen Titeln unabdingbar. Mit dieser Karte kann man sich und einander einschätzen und weiss, wo wer in dieser Hierarchie steht. Auch je nachdem wie man sich kleidet, wird man eingestuft.

– – Sie haben viel von mir verlangt, aber auch viel von sich selber.

– – Doch, ich freute mich immer auf meine Arbeit in Süd-Korea. Ich konnte viel geben, habe aber auch viel bekommen.

– – Korea ist kein Land für jedermann, wenn man sich nicht an die folgenden Regeln halten kann. Man muss immer bereit sein für Änderungen und sich schnell anpassen können. Man muss Seltsames essen können, das meiste davon sehr scharf gewürzt. Man sollte Abenteuer geniessen und das Unerwartete erwarten. Man sollte dem Volk vertrauen und versuchen sie zu verstehen. Man sollte ihre Vorschläge akzeptieren und nicht meinen man wisse mehr als sie. Sie können uns, in ihrem Land, mehr helfen als wir ihnen. Wenn man sich anpassen kann, und nach den koreanischen Sitten leben kann, wird man eine interessante und spannende Zeit in diesem „Land der Morgen-Ruhe", wie Süd-Korea genannt wird, erleben.

Danke schön! Kam-sa-ham-ni-da!

Oster-Abendmahl Vorbereitung

Jetzt sind wir in der Passionszeit und wir bereiten uns für die Auferstehung Jesu Christi vor. Wenn wir uns auch dieses Jahr Karfreitag und Ostern nähern, denken wir wieder daran, wie Jesus für uns gelitten hat. Wir erinnern uns auch an das Abendessen, als er zusammen mit seinen Jüngern zum letzten Mal, bevor er gekreuzigt wurde, ass. Was wollte Jesus eigentlich mit dieser Feier?

Was hier folgt ist eine Eucharistie-Liturgie und ein Versuch zu erklären, was Jesus von diesem Abendmahl erhoffte. Wenn wir das Abendmahl jetzt miteinander zelebrieren, versuchen wir es anders zu verstehen, eine tiefere oder wirklichere Bedeutung zu erlangen.

Abendmahl-Liturgie:

Jetzt sind wir all eingeladen zum Mahl des Herrn. Wenn jemand nicht daran teilnehmen kann oder will, so ist er doch freundlich eingeladen bei uns zu bleiben und so in der Stille teilzuhaben an unserer Gemeinschaft.

Eingang:

Liebe Mitchristen! Unser Herr, Jesus Christus, hat das Mahl bereitet für die, welche hungern und dürsten nach seiner Gerechtigkeit, in der er Leben und reiche Fülle schenkt. Wir wollen uns mit dem verbünden, der uns über bitten und verstehen hinaus aufrichten und reich machen kann und will. In diesen Tagen werden wir in besonderer Weise an die Gegenwart des Auferstandenen erinnert und in seine Gemeinschaft gerufen.

Gebet:

Lieber Gott, wir kommen zu diesem Tisch nicht im Vertrauen auf unsere Tugend, denn wir wissen, wie wir das Leben, zu dem du uns rufst, verfehlt haben und verfehlen. Wir vertrauen nur auf deine Liebe. Du speisest uns nicht mit Überresten von deinem Tisch ab. Du willst uns als Gäste an deinem Tisch haben. Für diese Liebe danken wir dir. Gib, dass deine Gaben uns ernähren und erhalten zum ewigen Leben. Lass uns in dir Leben und reiche Fülle finden. Amen.

Schriftlesung: Jeremia 31:31-34 (Hebräer8:7-13)

„Gibt acht! Es kommt die Zeit, da will ich einen neuen Bund schliessen mit dem Haus Israel und dem Haus Juda, ungleich dem alten Bund, den ich mit ihren Vätern schloss, als ich sie an der Hand nahm und sie aus Ägypten führte, dem Bund, den sie nicht hielten, obgleich ich ihr Herr war. So soll der Bund sein, den ich mit dem Haus Israel schliesse nach dieser Zeit, spricht der Herr: Ich lege meine Gesetz in ihr Herz und schreibe es in ihren Sinn, sie sollen mein Volk, ich will ihr Gott sein. Da wird keiner den andern lehren und sagen: „Erkenne den Herrn!“ Denn sie alle werden mich kennen, Kleine und Grosse. Ihre Untaten will ich vergeben und ihrer Sünde nicht mehr gedenken.“ (nach Jörg Zink)

Im Abendmahl wird dieser neue Bund verwirklicht. Aber was ist der Bund? Wie ist Christus gegenwärtig in Brot und Wein?

Weisung:

Während des letzten Mahles mit den Jüngern nahm Jesus das Brot, dankte Gott dafür, brach es in Stücke, gab es seinen Jüngern mit den Worten: „Nehmt und esst, das ist mein Leib, der für euch zerbrochen wird. Tut das (auch in Zukunft) zur Erinnerung an mich!"

Jesus war wirklicher Mensch. Er lebte in der Geschichte und wanderte über diese Erde. Er selber, ganz, gibt sich uns im Zeichen von Brot mit allem, was sein Wesen umfasst. Indem wir uns im Abendmahl an ihn erinnern lassen, sollen wir ihn annehmen als unseren Herrn und Befreier. Eben jetzt will er uns seine Gemeinschaft schenken, so dass wir ihm nachfolgen können.

Dann nahm Jesus bei jenem Mahl den Becher, sprach das Dankgebet und sagte: „Trinkt alle daraus; das ist mein Blut, das für euch vergossen wird zur Vergebung der Schuld. Dieser Becher ist der neue Bund (und Versprechen) Gottes, der durch mein Blut besiegelt wird."

Jesus wusste, dass er gekreuzigt würde. Er gab sich selbst hin zur Erlösung für viele. Das war der Wille seines Vaters, unseres Gottes. Durch seinen Tod, machte er den Gottesbund wirksam. Durch diesen Bund wird uns bedingungslos Vergebung angeboten. Wenn wir sie annehmen, empfangen wir selber die Kraft zur Vergebung und zur tragfähigen Liebe, mit der wir unseren Nächsten entgegenkommen und ihre menschliche Eigenart achten wollen.

Wenn wir jetzt zu seinem Mahle kommen, soll sich jedes fragen. „Was will Gott mir persönlich durch Jesus Christus schenken? Bedenken wir noch einmal: Gott will uns durch dieses Mahl nicht nur ein wenig erheben und trösten, sondern er will uns das Leben und reiche Fülle schenken. Unser ganzes Wesen wird neu belebt. Dies erfahren wir besonders, wenn wir das Neue ins tägliche Leben bringen. Indem wir uns die Einladung an seinen Tisch gefallen lassen, bekennen wir: "Ja, Gott, ich nehme deine Vergebung an. Ich weiss, dass ich von dir angenommen bin. Ich glaube, Herr, hilf meinem Unglauben!"

Jesus wollte mit dem Letzten Mahl nicht erreichen, dass wir ihn anbeten, sondern dass wir unser Leben nach seinem Leben führen, nicht nur mit Worten, sondern auch mit Taten. Er wollte also, dass wir für unsere Mitmenschen leben!

Gebet:

O Herr, wir danken dir, dass wir in deinem Sohne Vergebung finden für unsere Schuld. Wir danken dir, dass du in ihm auch Herr bist über unsere Gegenwart und Zukunft, so dass unser Leben Sinn bekommt. In diesem Mahl bekennen wir uns zu dir: Wir wollen dir angehören mit Leib, Seele und Geist. Schenke uns die Kraft der Vergebung, die Geduld des Verständnisses und eine tragfähige Liebe. Führe du uns selber ins gemeinsame Leben.

Einladung, Einsetzen und Austeilung:

Immer wenn wir diese Mahlgemeinschaft feiern, denken wir an das, was Jesus für die ganze Menschheit durch seinen Tod ermöglicht hat.

Gebet:

Lieber Gott, du hast uns durch Brot und Wein versichert, dass du bei uns bist und bleibst. Du hast uns in deinen Bund eingeschlossen und uns Vergebung geschenkt. Hilf, dass wir uns von dir verbünden lassen und gib, dass wir mithelfen können, dass auch andere über deinem Bunde froh werden. Lieber Herr, wir beten jetzt miteinander das Gebet, das du die Jünger gelehrt hast. Erhöre uns!

Unser Vater im Himmel, geheiligt werde dein Name. Dein Reich komme. Dein Wille geschehe wie im Himmel, so auf Erden. Unser tägliches Brot gib uns heute. Und vergib uns unsere Schuld, wie auch wir vergeben unseren Schuldigen. Und führe uns nicht in Versuchung, sondern erlöse uns von dem Bösen. Denn dein ist das Reich und die Kraft und die Herrlichkeit in Ewigkeit. Amen. (Ökumenische Fassung)

Sendung:

Nachdem die Jünger ein Lied gesungen hatten, verliessen sie den oberen Raum und gingen still und nachdenklich hinaus. So wollen wir nun auch still hinausgehen und dem nachdenken, was uns geschenkt worden ist.

Segen:

Gott unser Schöpfer,
Christus Jesus unser Fürsprecher,
der Heilige Geist unser Helfer
segne uns und gebe uns Frieden zu allen Zeiten. Amen.

Schuldbekenntnis

Pfarrer:	Wir bekennen unsere Schuld.
Gemeinde/Pfarrer:	Gott unser Vater, wir öffnen unser Leben vor Dir in aller Ehrlichkeit.
Pfarrer:	Du siehst unsere nützlichen Taten, unsere Ziele, die wir noch nicht erreicht haben;
Gemeinde:	unsere Mutlosigkeit, wenn wir unseren Mitmenschen, um die wir besorgt sind, nicht helfen können.
Pfarrer:	Ja, und Du siehst auch, wenn wir Böses getan haben;
Gemeinde:	wenn wir uns nicht um unsere Mitmenschen gekümmert haben, denen wir Liebe geben sollten;
Pfarrer:	wenn wir den Schrei des Notleidenden nicht haben hören wollen;
Gemeinde:	wenn wir unsere Mitmenschen missachten oder sogar hassen.
Pfarrer:	Gott der Einheit, Gott der Ganzheit, wir bekennen, dass wir manchmal sehr allein leben aber das beschäftigt uns.
Gemeinde:	Die Welt ist voll von Menschen, vor denen wir Angst haben.
Pfarrer:	Wir haben Angst vor uns selber, und wir fürchten Dich.
Gemeinde:	Deshalb versuchen wir in unserem eigenen Wesen eine Welt zu erschaffen und darin ganz allein zu leben.
Pfarrer:	Aber wir ersticken vor Enttäuschung und Einsamkeit.
Gemeinde:	Wir suchen verzweifelt nach einem besseren Verständnis unserer Selbst.
Pfarrer:	Wir sehnen uns danach, die Leute besser kennenzulernen, mit denen wir leben.
Gemeinde/Pfarrer:	Wir brauchen den Mut Deiner Liebe, O Gott, um uns aus unserem eigenen Gefängnis zu befreien und um auch andere frei zu machen.
Pfarrer:	Herr, durch Deine Liebe entlasse uns aus dieser Knechtschaft und den künstlichen Vorbildern, die wir haben.
Gemeinde:	Vergib uns unsere Unzulänglichkeit.
Gemeinde /Pfarrer:	Mach uns zu Deinen Mitarbeitern, um die Welt zur vollen Menschlichkeit zu führen, durch Christus Jesus, unseren Herr. AMEN

Zuspruch

Pfarrer:	Seid getrost, fürchtet Euch nicht! Denn es sollen wohl Berge weichen und Hügel hinfallen, aber meine Gnade soll nicht von Dir weichen, und der Bund meines Friedens soll nicht hinfallen, spricht der Herr, Dein Erbarmer.
Gemeinde:	Dafür danken wir Dir, Gott.
Pfarrer:	Wenn Christus in einem Menschen ist, wird er ein ganz und gar neues Wesen; die Vergangenheit ist beendet und vorbei, alles ist jetzt und neu.
Gemeinde:	Weil wir denn diese Verheissung haben, so vertrauen wir, dass wir durch seine Gnade von aller Schuld erlöst werden.
Pfarrer:	Gottes Barmherzigkeit hört nie auf; ich sage Euch im Namen Jesu Christi, **Uns ist vergeben!**

Warum lässt Gott das zu?

An die Ostermundigen Konfirmandinnen und Konfirmanden, Mai 1994:

In den Glaubenssätzen, die ich von Euch Konfirmandinnen und Konfirmanden gegen Schluss des Konfirmandenjahres verlange, kommt es oftmals vor, dass Ihr an Gott zweifelt. Ihr schreibt „Gibt es wirklich einen Gott? Wenn es doch einen gäbe, warum lässt er so viel Ungerechtigkeit, Krieg und Folter zu? Warum verhungern so viele Menschen in der Welt? Warum lässt Gott zu, dass unsere Natur zerstört wird? Gott, wenn du ein liebender, barmherziger Gott bist, solltest du alles gut machen." Diese Fragen und andere ähnliche habt Ihr gestellt, und solche Fragen werden immer wieder auch von Erwachsenen gestellt. Wie können wir diese berechtigten Fragen beantworten?

Ich denke, wir sind nicht eine Laune, ein Zufallsprodukt der Natur. Wir alle sind auf die Welt gestellt, weil ein Plan vor uns liegt. Aber, ob wir den Plan verwirklichen? Gott steht uns bei und hilft uns doch diesen Plan zu realisieren. Gott will nur das Beste für uns. Warum dann, wenn das so ist, lässt er so viel Elend in der Welt zu? Wenn wir in unserer Gruppe versuchen einander zu verstehen, ohne an unseren egoistischen Ideen festzuhalten, kann das auch ansteckend sein. Hier fängt Frieden an!

Liebe Konfirmandinnen, liebe Konfirmanden, wenn wir zur Natur keine Sorge tragen, weil wir dazu zu bequem oder zu gedankenlos sind, was dann?—Zigarettenstummel aus dem Autofenster werfen, oder sogar Aschenbecher am Boden ausleeren, Papier und Büchsen im Wald zurücklassen, chemische Dünger und Schneckengift im Garten ausstreuen, mit bleihaltigem Benzin und ohne Katalysator fahren usw.

Wir können natürlich nichts dafür, wenn eine Naturkatastrophe geschieht. Wenn wir z.B. ein Erdbeben erleben, können wir es kaum verhindern. Doch mit immer Öl und andere Bodenschätze aus der Erde nehmen, verursachen wir im Erdboden Hohlräume, was Erdbeben mitverursachen kann. Denken wir auch an die Erdwärme, wie viele Naturschäden wir verursachen. Luftverunreinigung durch Fabrikrauch und Abgase von Autos und Flugzeugen ist auch ein Problem für unsere Umwelt. Wenn hunderte Menschen getötet werden, weil ein grosses Gebäude, das nicht nach Vorschriften gebaut wurde, zusammenkracht, dann ist doch der Architekt des Gebäudes, der unehrlich Geld gespart und verdient hat, der Schuldige, sagen wir; aber wir sind auch mitschuldig, wenn wir beim Kauf des Gebäudes sparen konnten oder wir weniger Mietzins bezahlen, oder sonst anders profitieren können. Wir haben wieder bloss an uns gedacht. Sicher finden wir viele ähnliche Beispiele.

Die Schweiz ist ein reiches Land und niemand muss hier verhungern. Doch in anderen Teilen der Welt leidet die Bevölkerung ungeheuerlich. Wenn wir Menschen in diesem Land und in anderen Ländern den Hungernden helfen wollten und würden, ohne dass jeder nur an sich selber, an seinen Geldbeutel oder an seine eventuell zu verlierende Zeit denkt, könnten wir alle viel mehr für unsere Mitmenschen tun.

Ist es uns bewusst, dass z.B. die Schweiz in den letzten Jahren durchschnittlich rund acht Milliarden Franken pro Jahr an der 3.-Welt verdient hat und als Hilfe für diese Entwicklungsländer leistet sie einen Beitrag von etwa einer halben Milliarde Franken pro Jahr.

Liebe Mitchristen, Gott steht uns bei und hilft uns, aber er tut unsere Arbeit nicht. „Gott hat keine Hände, nur unsere Hände, um seine Arbeit zu tun." Wenn unsere Hände mit anderen Dingen als mit den seinen beschäftigt sind, was dann?

Es wäre sicher langweilig und keine Herausforderung, wenn Gott für uns alles in Ordnung bringen und erledigen würde. Wir müssten keine Sorge mehr tragen. Nur dasitzen und nichts machen oder das tun, was wir wollten, ohne an unsere Freunde, Familien, Bekannten, Mitmenschen, die Natur oder an die Zukunft zu denken. Alles kommt sowieso gut. Wenn es so wäre, dann würden wir sagen, „Gott, du bist ungerecht! Warum dürfen wir keine Entscheidungen treffen?! Hast du kein Vertrauen in uns?! Wir wollen auch mitbestimmen dürfen, was auf der Erde geschieht!"

Um die Frage „Warum lässt Gott das zu?" beantworten zu können, merken wir dass wir Menschen selber vielfach, direkt oder indirekt, für das Elend in der Welt verantwortlich sind.

Wir besinnen uns, „Selig sind, die da Leid tragen, denn sie sollen getröstet werden" (Mt. 5,4) und „So werden die Letzten die Ersten sein und die Ersten die Letzten." (Mt. 20,16)

10 Jahre Jubiläum - Lidopark, 27. 8. 2014, 10.45 Uhr, in der Kapelle

Thema: Das Alter

Heute feiern wir Geburtstag, - - 10 Jahre Lidopark! Eigentlich 10 Jahre sind nicht viel, wenn wir vom Menschenleben sprechen. Das 10-jährige persönliche Jubiläum haben wir alle überschritten. Jung sind wir nicht mehr!

Oft meinen wir, mit dem Altwerden ist man langsam mit dem Leben fertig. Jungsein, das ist das Höchste; jung wollen wir bleiben!

Junge Frauen sind hübsch; junge Männer sind stark! Diese Menschen stehen in der Blüte des Lebens; sie denken schnell; sie sehen und hören gut; sie können helfen die Welt zu verändern. Alte Leute können nicht mehr so viel, - - oder so denken wir manchmal! Nachdem wir unsere Kinder grossgezogen haben, vielleicht auch Enkel und Urenkel, und der Mann ins Pensionsalter kommt, ist das Leben vorüber. Wir haben gewiss weniger Verantwortung, oder besser gesagt, andere Verantwortung.

Körperlich fehlt uns die Kraft, soviel wie früher zu leisten. Aber vorüber ist das Leben nicht, - - nur wenn wir so meinen! Diesen Schock, „Altsein", gilt es zu besiegen, nicht zu überspielen; „JA" zu sagen zu dieser neuen Lebenslage; diese frische Lebensstufe anzunehmen.

Daraus ergeben sich positive Erkenntnisse: Vollkommen brauchen wir nicht zu sein; Fehler dürfen wir machen. Unter einem starken Leistungsdruck stehen wir nicht mehr. Also, was wir jetzt tun, macht uns hoffentlich Spass und Freude, und darum gelingt es uns auch. Freiwillig können wir zunehmend unsere Kräfte einsetzen.

Die Bibel, Sacharja 14:7, umschreibt den Abend am Tag des Herrn mit den Worten: „Um den Abend wird es licht sein". D.h. am Abend unseres Lebens kann es hell sein. Diese Seite des Alters gilt es zu sehen, und zur Geltung zu bringen, wie Udo Jürgens weiss, wenn er singt: „Mit 66 Jahren fängt das Leben an, mit 66 Jahren hat man Spass daran".

Wichtig ist die Bereitschaft, Erfahrungen weiterzugeben. Gewiss muss jede Generation ihre eigenen Erfahrungen sammeln, aber das entbindet sie nicht von der Aufgabe, der jüngeren Generation Hilfen anzubieten, auf Gefahren hinzuweisen, Wege und Irrwege aufzuzeigen. So können wir Wegweiser sein, damit unsere Kinder wissen, wohin der Weg führt, den sie gehen. Aber hören sie uns? Damit sie zuhören, ist es unsere Aufgabe, die Weisheiten deutlich und bescheiden weiter zu geben. Entscheidungen können wir ihnen nicht abnehmen. Selber müssen sie wählen.

Doch können junge Menschen auch etwas anbieten, indem sie ihre älteren Mitmenschen mit neuen Ideen vertraut machen. Auch sie dürfen angehört werden. In den technischen Dingen z.B. lasse ich mich gerne beraten, weil die heutige Technik weit fortgeschrittener ist als in meiner, in unserer Jugend. Meine Kinder wissen u.a. viel mehr über PCs und solche Elektronik als ich. Unsere Pflicht ist es, auch ihr Wissen zu berücksichtigen.

Junge Menschen haben Ehrgeiz und wollen Veränderung. Alte Leute haben Weisheit, und wollen eine stabile Welt. Also benötigt die Welt junge und alte Menschen: Menschen mit Ehrgeiz, und Menschen mit Wertbeständigkeit; Menschen mit neuen Ideen, und die mit Erfahrung; Menschen mit Schaffenskraft, und die mit Besonnenheit. Dadurch wird das nötige Gleichgewicht in unserer Welt hergestellt.

Je älter ich werde, desto deutlicher erkenne ich Gottes Fügungen, die mein Leben entscheidend beeinflusst haben: meine Jugendzeit in einer christlichen Familie; Arbeit auf einem Ölbohrturm in Alaska, mit hart gesottenen Männern; Biologiestudium und wissenschaftliche Arbeit mit der „Fisch und Wild Verwaltung" in Alaska, in dieser Zeit u.a. auf einem japanischen Fischerboot; Wechsel von Biologie zu Theologie; eine Frau, Kinder, Umzug in die Schweiz; neue Sprache; andere Menschen; drei Pfarrämter; gute und schlechte Erlebnisse; Curling spielen; Reisen in Nah- und Fernost; Outback in Australien; Überall in Afrika; in einem Gummiboot durch den Grand Canyon auf dem Colorado Fluss; meine mehr-jährige Pfarrarbeit in Süd-Korea; und nun Lidopark.

Durch all diese Jahre habe ich ständige Kontakte mit Menschen und Kulturen. Mit solchen Früchten werde ich tagtäglich reifer. Wir haben alle, jeden Tag, Erlebnisse, die uns reifer machen, aber nicht die gleichen. Das macht das Leben interessant und spannend. Durch diese Erfahrungen und gesammelten Weisheiten sind wir alle fähig die Sichten unserer Mitmenschen zu erweitern.

Ebenso wichtig ist, unsere eigenen Fähigkeiten für uns persönlich einzusetzen. Denken wir doch an das, was wir noch vollbringen und anbieten können.

Mit dem Älterwerden bekommt man mehr Zeit zum Nachdenken, Beobachten, Lesen, Spazieren oder sogar Sport treiben; sich dem Augenblick widmen, geniessen, entdecken; sich über kleine Dinge der Gegenwart freuen; da sein für Kinder und Enkel: spielen, zuhören, Geschichten erzählen. Ob Grosseltern den Enkeln Bibelgeschichten erzählen, und ihnen das Beten näher bringen?

Das Alter braucht nicht untätig, passiv zu sein. Darum wird in Seniorenheimen, und anderswo gebastelt, geturnt, gesungen, gekegelt, gejasst, getanzt und gekocht. Auch Vorträge und Gespräche regen den Geist an. „Wer rastet, der rostet"; das gilt ebenso für das Alter.

Gegen Einsamkeit und Verbitterung hilft die Erfüllung kleiner Aufgaben und Pflichten. Hier in Lidopark haben wir alle diese Möglichkeiten. Wir dürfen und sollen sie nutzen, um jung zu bleiben, und das Alter zu geniessen.

Wir können unserer Gesellschaft Interessantes anbieten, und dadurch das Leben unseren Mitmenschen, auch hier in Lidopark, wertvoller machen helfen. Ein freundliches oder lächelndes Gesicht ausstrahlen bereitet den Menschen Freude. Das macht auch unser Leben angeregt und wertvoll. Durch solche persönlichen Einsätze und Merkmale helfen wir uns selber, und den anderen.

Positives Denken ist sicher wichtig. Nicht denken: „dafür bin ich zu alt; das kann ich sowieso nicht mehr", sondern froh sein über das, was ich noch tun kann. Wenn man <u>will</u> oder <u>muss</u> kann man viel mehr, als was man denkt.

Pensionierte Ehepaare haben mehr Zeit für- und miteinander etwas zu tun: gemeinsame Ausflüge und Reisen unternehmen, ein Essen auswärts, das Arbeit spart und Spass macht, da man dies früher vielleicht nicht so oft tat.

Es gibt noch so viele Dinge, über die man sich freuen darf. Ich weiss, dass ältere Leute manchmal denken, dies oder jenes Geschenk brauchten sie nicht mehr. Aber es ist doch schön, wenn jemand uns beschenkt, und wir dann etwas Neues benützen oder ansehen dürfen. Menschen freuen sich, wenn ihre Geschenke angenommen werden.

Ich schliesse mit einem Herbst Bild:

Wie die Früchte zum Reifen auf die Herbstsonne angewiesen sind, so sind ältere Menschen, wir alle, auf Wärme, Geborgenheit und Liebe angewiesen. Sie sind in dem Eingebundensein in einer Familie, Hausgemeinschaft, Nachbarschaft, Freundeskreis und ganz besonders hier in Lidopark, das überdies Möglichkeiten zu Begegnungen schafft.

Die Initiative muss doch von zwei Seiten kommen: Einladungen von aussen, wie auch hier heute, und die eigene Bereitschaft, sich aus der Isolierung herauszuholen und neuen Herausforderungen entgegen zu gehen. Dann ist im Alter Freude und erfülltes Leben.

Diese Erfüllung wird in der Bibel beschrieben, nach Sirach 25,3-6: Dein Alter ist wie deine Jugend. Hilfreicher Rat passt zu weissem Haar. Weisheit, Besonnenheit und Einsicht, erwartet man von alten Menschen. Ihre Krone ist ihre Erfahrung.

Und nicht vergessen:

Es kommt nicht darauf an, wie alt man wird, sondern wie man alt wird!

Mit diesen Worten möchte ich Ihnen Mut machen, in die Zukunft zu blicken, Ihr Leben neu anzuschauen, und vielleicht nochmals neu zu gestalten.

Gebet:

Lieber Gott, hilf uns einem wertvollen, nützlichen und erfüllten Leben in den nächsten Jahren entgegen zu gehen. Amen.

Danke, liebe Leute. Ich wünsche Euch allen weiterhin einen schönen Tag!

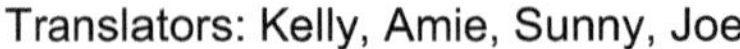

Translators: Kelly, Amie, Sunny, Joe

Acknowledgements

I wish to express my deepest appreciation to all those Koreans who showed me their nation in so many ways and assisted me in having such a wonderful time in Korea. I was able to collect so many impressions of this beautiful country and learn many customs. I was constantly exposed to new ideas and different concepts, sometimes quite challenging but also profitable to me. Through many accounts and frequent excursions on which I was taken, I experienced many Korean lifestyles and traditions. I came to greatly appreciate their culture, established over many centuries, and its importance in their contemporary way of life and the values by which they live.

I want especially to give my utmost thanks to Elder Jeong In-Chul (정 인철 장로), my very good friend, advisor, manager and Korean brother. He accompanied me during much of my time in Korea, organizing many activities including worship services throughout Korea and made it possible for me to see and take part in numerous events. I was able to travel with him on many of his missions and take part in many of his family happenings. I also thank his family members wholeheartedly for all their help and cordiality. Not only his family but many families have shown me their homes and let me be part of their daily lives.

Likewise I want to show my gratitude to my three main interpreters who translated my sermons form English to Korean. They are: Amie Song (송 연주), Sunny Lee (이 대선) and Joseph Kim (김 일조). If it had not been for them my many Korean Worship services would not have been possible.

I wish to thank Koo Kyeong-Ok (구 경구) cordially for taking time out of her busy life as wife and mother, to translate the two Korean sermons in this book. Both sermons also appear in English in this manuscript.

Furthermore I am extremely indebted to my two efficient proof readers, who spent countless hours reading and rereading my texts, and making suggestions, Ursula Norton Boss and my wife Mary Louise Norton. Leslie Kerr of Anchorage, Alaska was very helpful in the final proof reading and making valuable recommendations.

Jeong In-Chul was the most important person in my over fifteen active years in S. Korea"

About the Author

Thomas Norton, born in 1942, was a resident of Anchorage from 1949 until 1969 and attended Anchorage schools, then studied Biology in Alaska and Oregon. In San Anselmo, California, he graduated from San Francisco Theological Seminary with a Bachelor of Divinity in 1969 and a Master of Divinity in 1970. After moving to Switzerland in 1973, he earned a Verbi Divini Minister degree at the University of Bern. While studying theology he learned the German language and then was a Swiss pastor in the Canton of Bern for 30 years.

The Alaska Department Fish and Game employed Norton five summers, while he was attending university and seminary. His many Fish and Game adventures included a period as a fishery technician and customs officer on a Japanese fishing vessel in Prince William Sound. Biology continues to be one of his main interests.

In 2000, during his four-month sabbatical leave from his Swiss church, Norton went to South Korea and functioned in the mission field. He made a 25-minute video (English and German) of the activities in the "Island Medical Missionary (Presbyterian Church of Korea)", including information and pictures of its surrounding countryside. The Salvation Ship, operating out of the Mission Center on Palgum Island, visited and gave medical and spiritual care to the inhabitants on the many islands in southeast S. Korea.

During the summer of 2004, Thomas Norton attended a five-week Korean language (Hangul) course at Yonsei University (연세대학교) in Seoul.

After his early retirement in 2005, he went back to South Korea and was Pastor for English Ministry in Shin Kwang Presbyterian Church (신광 교회) in Seong Nam, adjacent to Seoul. He also pastored a short time in Mokpo in the Yang Dong Jee Il Presbyterian Church (양동재일 꾱회). During his pastoring, he kept in touch with the "Island Medical Missionary (PCK)".

He has spoken to churches and at events throughout S. Korea, including the world's largest reformed church, the Myung Sung Presbyterian Church (명성교회) in Seoul.

During Norton's ministry in Switzerland, he enjoyed the sport of curling and was a Swiss American Society member for more than thirty years. For six of those years he was president, thus having many embassy and other interesting contacts. In the past few years he has written about his youth in Alaska and several Fish and Game adventures.

In addition to their love of travel, Tom and his wife Mary value fitness, home, and family. They enjoy their many relatives in Switzerland, Alaska, Washington, Oregon, California and Missouri. They also like entertaining dinner guests. Tom and Mary continue to live in Switzerland.

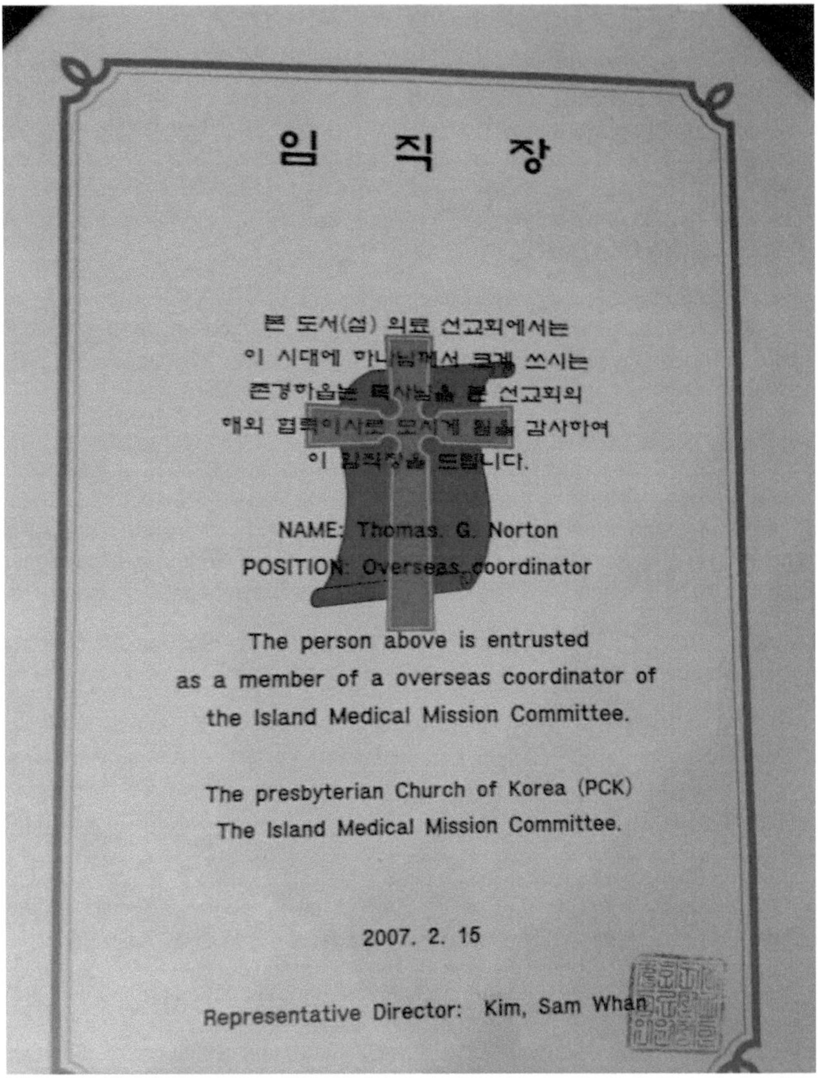

임 직 장

본 도서(섬) 의료 선교회에서는
이 시대에 하나님께서 크게 쓰시는
존경하옵는 목사님을 본 선교회의
해외 협력이사로 모시게 됨을 감사하여
이 임직장을 드립니다.

NAME: Thomas. G. Norton
POSITION: Overseas coordinator

The person above is entrusted
as a member of a overseas coordinator of
the Island Medical Mission Committee.

The presbyterian Church of Korea (PCK)
The Island Medical Mission Committee.

2007. 2. 15

Representative Director: Kim, Sam Whan

영어 성경 공부반
ENGLISH
Bible
Study
강사
T mas G. Norton
- 미국 알라스카 앵크리지 출생
- 앵크리지 감리교 대학교
- 조오지 폭스대학 졸업(B.S)
- 샌프란시스코 신학교(B.D, M.D)
- 샌프란시스코의 퍼시픽 메디컬 센타에서 임상목회
- 베른대학교(스위스)(VDM)
- 스위스의 개혁교회에서 목회함 (1975–지금까지)
- 현 신광교회 영어사역 담당
모집대상
1. 유소년부
· 일시 : 매주일 오전 10시 청년부실
· 대상 : 초등학생
· 개강 : 2006년 4월 2일(주일)
2. 중고등부
· 일시 : 매주일 오전 10시30분 청년부실
· 대상 : 중고등부
· 개강 : 2006년 4월 2일(주일)
3. 청년부
· 일시 : 매주일 오후 3시30분 청년부실
· 대상 : 청년
· 개강 : 2006년 4월 2일(주일)
4. 토요일 반
· 일시 : 매주토요일 오후4시–5시 청년부실
· 대상 : 원하는 사람 누구나
· 개강 : 2006년 5월 6일(토)
BIBLE
Bible
대/한/예/수/교/장/로/회
신광교회
담임목사 이 명 중
462-838 경기도 성남시 중원구 하대원동 106-1
전화 ☎ 031)752-2603~5 FAX : 721-4393
www.sk-church.or.kr
교회약도
서울
수진동
상남동
성당
신광교회

English
Bible Study
& Fun Games
Jesus
원어민 강사 :토마스 노튼 목사님
3/11~
6/ 3 매주 일요일
*유소년부 : 주일 아침 9시 -영어성경
*중고등부 : 주일 아침 9시 -영어성경
*성 인 부 : 주일 오후4시30분 -회화, 성령
장소: 성남 신광교회 교육관
"수강료 무료" 자세한 사항은 신광교회로 문의하여 주시기 바랍니다
대한예수교 장로회 성남 신광교회 (031-752-2603~5) / 영어담당 : 이대선 (011-9282-2603)
463-838 성남시 중원구 하대원동 105-1

Printed by Books on Demand GmbH, Norderstedt / Germany